Gloria Estefan

Superstar of Song

SALLY LEE

Enslow Publishers, Inc.

40 Industrial Road	PO Box 38
Box 398	Aldershot
Berkeley Heights, NJ 07922	Hants GU12 6BP
USA	UK

http://www.enslow.com

Library of Congress Cataloging-in-Publication Data

Lee, Sally.
    Gloria Estefan : superstar of song / Sally Lee.
      p. cm. — (Latino biography library)
    Includes bibliographical references and index.
    Discography: p.
    Videography: p.
    ISBN 0-7660-2490-3 (hardcover)
    1. Estefan, Gloria—Juvenile literature. 2. Singers—United States—Biography—Juvenile
literature. I. Title. II. Series.
    ML3930.E85L44 2005
    782.42164'092—dc22

                                            2004017140

Printed in the United States of America

10 9 8 7 6 5 4 3 2 1

To Our Readers: We have done our best to make sure all Internet Addresses in this book were active and appropriate when we went to press. However, the author and the publisher have no control over and assume no liability for the material available on those Internet sites or on other Web sites they may link to. Any comments or suggestions can be sent by e-mail to comments@enslow.com or to the address on the back cover.

Every effort has been made to locate all copyright holders of material used in this book. If any errors or omissions have occurred, corrections will be made in future editions of this book.

Illustration Credits: AP/Wide World, pp. 1, 3, 4, 6, 9, 12, 16, 38, 40–41, 48, 53, 60, 63, 67, 71, 74–75, 79, 80, 88, 91, 94, 101, 104; Artville, LLC, p. 14; Classmates.com, p. 25; Estefan Enterprises, pp. 20, 23, 34; Miami Herald, p. 32; Private Collection, p. 47; Raul Demolina/Shooting Star, p. 57.

Cover Illustration: AP/Wide World.

Contents

1. A Haunting Fear   5

2. "No Children, No Pets,
   No Cubans"   13

3. Prince Charming   27

4. The Machine
   Starts Rolling   37

5. Crossover!   45

6. Letting It Loose   55

7. Coming Out of the Dark   66

8. An American Head
   and a Cuban Heart   72

9. Reaching Higher   84

10. Giving Back   96

Chronology   108

Discography   111

Videography   113

Chapter Notes   114

Further Reading with
Internet Addresses   125

Index   126

Gloria Estefan

1

A Haunting Fear

Just when it seemed as if life could not get any better for Gloria Estefan, the call came. The president of the United States wanted to see her at the White House. Gloria was thrilled.[1] She had come a long way from Cuba, the homeland she had fled with her parents when she was a toddler. She was no longer the shy teenager who did most of her singing alone in her bedroom. By 1990 Estefan had become an international singing star.

In the spring of 1990, Gloria Estefan made her memorable visit to the White House. Her husband, Emilio, and nine-year-old son, Nayib, were with her. They sat in the Oval Office chatting with President George H. W. Bush, the father of future president George W. Bush. Although Estefan was famous for her singing, that is not what earned her the presidential invitation. President Bush wanted to congratulate her for her

President H. W. Bush thanked Gloria for her ad campaign against drugs.

billboard campaign aimed at keeping young people off drugs.[2]

Estefan's White House visit came at a time when everything was going well for the pretty, dark-haired singer. By then she and her band, Miami Sound Machine, had sold 10 million albums worldwide. Her latest album, *Cuts Both Ways*, was an international success. Her concert tour had played to packed houses in Europe and the United States. Just weeks before, she had received a Golden Globe award, given to

Nayib Meets the President

When Gloria Estefan visited the White House with her family in 1990, she thought nine-year-old Nayib might be nervous about meeting President George H. W. Bush. But Nayib had no problem chatting with the president. He told President Bush how wonderful Mrs. Bush had been on the television special *Salute to American Teachers*. The president was charmed. Then President Bush brought out a fortune-telling ball and turned it upside down. He teased Nayib that it was used to make decisions at the White House. "You ask it a question and it says 'Yes, No, Maybe,'" Gloria laughed, recalling the president's explanation.[3]

performers who have sold more than 5 million albums outside the United States.

On the surface, Estefan's life seemed nearly perfect. But hidden deep in her mind was a gnawing fear that had haunted her since childhood. She worried that someday she would be disabled and be a burden to the people she loved. Her father had been ill for many years and required constant care from the rest of the family. Estefan was so afraid of following in his footsteps that she had insisted on installing an elevator in her new home.[4]

The morning after the White House visit, Estefan and her family boarded a luxurious tour bus in New York City for a five-hour trip to Syracuse, New York.

She chose to travel by bus because it would give her a chance to rest up for her strenuous performance that night.

"That day everything was perfect," Estefan said. "My husband and my son, Nayib, were with me. The tour had sold out everywhere. I was looking forward to the gig in Syracuse. And I loved the bus. I always used to say, if you crash, at least you're not falling 37,000 feet."[5]

Once the trip started, they all passed the time in their own way. Nayib and his tutor worked on his studies in the back of the bus. Emilio conducted business on his cell phone in the front. Gloria stretched out on a couch and watched an old spy movie on the VCR until she fell asleep. Snow was falling when the bus reached the Pocono Mountains in Pennsylvania. The bad weather was already causing problems for some drivers. Ahead of their bus, a tractor-trailer had skidded sideways, blocking all westbound lanes of the icy highway. The driver, Ron Jones, stopped the bus behind a truck loaded with copper coils, and waited for the highway to clear.

Moments later, a tractor-trailer carrying nineteen tons of fruit came over the crest of a hill.[6] The driver saw the stopped traffic ahead. He stepped on his brakes, but something went terribly wrong. The brakes failed. The tractor-trailer picked up speed as it raced down the hill. There was no place for the runaway truck to go. It crashed into the back of the bus, slamming it forward into the stopped truck.

The impact was explosive. Gloria was hurled onto the floor of the bus. Emilio was knocked completely out of his tennis shoes. His feet were cut by broken glass as he ran back to check on his wife and son. "Baby, are you all right?" he cried.[7]

"I think I broke my back," Gloria answered.[8] Emilio tried to reassure her by suggesting that she had just pulled a muscle.[9] But Gloria knew differently. She lay on the floor in agonizing pain. The performer known for her high-energy singing and dancing could barely move her legs. As she lay on the floor of the bus, she remembered her haunting fear. "Here it is," she thought. "This is the thing I've been waiting for."[10]

"That day was perfect," said Estefan—until her tour bus crashed in a terrible accident.

Like any mother, Gloria's first concern was for her child. Emilio found him on the floor in the back of the bus covered with shoes, bags, and other items. Nayib complained of a sore shoulder, but he was not seriously hurt.

Gloria lay on her back in agonizing pain. A metallic taste tingled in her mouth. She knew her back was broken. She also knew that the slightest move could cause more damage. Gloria lay still and concentrated on a spot on the ceiling to try to take her mind off the pain. Nayib sat by his mother and held her hand as they comforted each other during the long wait for an ambulance. "Gloria appeared to be in terrible pain," said Nayib's tutor, Lori Rooney. "But her only concern was to make sure Nayib thought she was okay."[11]

> **"Here it is. This is the thing I've been waiting for."**
>
> **—Gloria Estefan**

The icy highway and blocked traffic hindered the paramedics from making the long drive from Scranton, Pennsylvania. It took more than an hour for them to reach the disabled bus. Estefan hoped they would give her something to ease her pain, but that did not happen. Medications could distort the results of tests she would need at the hospital. "The pain was almost unbearable as I was strapped to a board and carried through a hole that used to be the windshield," Estefan said. "I could feel the snow on my face and the people looking down at me with fear in their eyes."[12]

Estefan was taken to the Community Medical Center Regional Trauma Center in Scranton. After a series of tests, Dr. Harry Schmaltz delivered the bad news. Gloria had broken a vertebra, one of the bones in her back that protects the spine. "Another half inch of movement of the spine, she'd be completely paralyzed," said Dr. Schmaltz.[13] Emilio fainted on hearing the news.

After discussing treatment options with the doctors, Gloria and Emilio decided surgery would give her the best chance of regaining full movement of her back. Still, surgery was risky and could result in serious infection or even permanent paralysis. Emilio called everyone he knew to get recommendations for a good back surgeon. He chose Dr. Michael Neuwirth at the Orthopedic Institute Hospital for Joint Diseases in New York City.

The next day, Emilio and Gloria flew by helicopter to New York City for the surgery. During the flight, Emilio thought about the long period of healing that lay ahead of them. Just then a ray of sunshine broke through the clouds and poured into the helicopter. This shaft of light would later inspire a song, "Coming Out of the Dark."[14]

Two days after her accident, Gloria was wheeled into the operating room. During the three-hour surgery, Dr. Neuwirth placed an eight-inch titanium rod on each side of Gloria's broken vertebra. The surgery left her with four hundred stitches and, later, a fourteen-inch scar.

The surgery was a success, and Estefan was leaving the hospital in New York City.

When Gloria woke up in the recovery room and saw Emilio's smiling face, she knew she was going to be okay.[15] "She's a wonderful patient," Dr. Neuwirth said after the surgery. "There is nothing prima donna-ish about her at all."[16]

On April 4, 1990, two weeks after the accident, Estefan was allowed to go home. A crowd of journalists and well-wishers gathered in front of the hospital to say goodbye. Estefan, seated in a wheelchair, surprised everyone by standing up. "No problem," she said with a smile. "Hopefully, in a few months, I will be back as good as new."[17]

If people were surprised by Gloria Estefan's courage, they should not have been. Her back may have been broken, but her spirit was as strong as ever. She knew that she had a long and painful rehabilitation ahead of her, but she was ready to take control and get her life back.

"No Children, No Pets, No Cubans"

When the Spanish explorer Christopher Columbus first arrived in Cuba, he wrote in his journal, "It is the most beautiful island ever seen."[1] But this beautiful country has a long history of political unrest. Many of its leaders have cared more about wealth and power than about the needs of their people.

One such leader was Fulgencio Batista. He was a dictator who carried out a military takeover to become Cuba's president in 1952. Batista arrived full of promises. In the end he had just replaced one corrupt government with another. Anyone who disagreed with any of his policies was imprisoned, tortured, or killed.

During Batista's presidency, the city of Havana became a playground for tourists, especially wealthy Americans. They were attracted to the lavish casinos, luxury hotels, and the drinking, gambling, and prostitution that went on there. American mobsters were

The island of Cuba is just ninety miles from Florida.

allowed to run these businesses as long as they shared their profits with Batista's government. Money poured into the country, but it never reached the majority of Cubans, who continued to live in poverty.

It was on this beautiful but troubled island of Cuba that Gloria Marie Fajardo was born on September 1, 1957. Her father, José Manuel Fajardo, was a tall athletic man who worked as a security guard for President Batista's family. Her mother, also named Gloria, was an intelligent and talented teacher. With two incomes, the Fajardos were able to lead a comfortable, middle-class life in Havana.

Glorita (Little Gloria) was a year old when another

political uprising occurred. A young lawyer and political revolutionary named Fidel Castro succeeded in over-throwing Batista. In the wee hours of January 1, 1959, Batista fled Cuba. Many of his followers left in such a hurry that they boarded planes still wearing their New Year's Eve party clothes.[2]

Castro set out to rid Cuba of Batista's supporters. He rounded up more than five hundred of the former dictator's top officials. Some were imprisoned, and others were executed by firing squads. Gloria's father was not rounded up, but he was hurt by his association with Batista. "He couldn't get a job anywhere," Gloria said later. "They wouldn't let him do anything. So he took us out."[3]

When Glorita was eighteen months old, her parents squeezed whatever belongings they could fit into a few suitcases. It had to look as if they were taking a trip—not fleeing from Castro. They bought round-trip tickets to Miami, Florida. Gloria's mother hoped to be there for only a couple of months.[4] The Fajardo family was stopped at the airport in Cuba. Officials searched their luggage and found the university diploma and teaching certificate Gloria's mother had tucked inside. The officials ripped up these documents so that Gloria's mother would not be able to use them to get a teaching job in the United States. Finally, the Fajardos were allowed to board the plane. Glorita was leaving Cuba, but her homeland would stay in her heart for the rest of her life.

Fidel Castro (in glasses) stands in front of a painting of General Batista on a horse.

Thousands of Cubans fled the country after Castro's revolution. Most of the refugees settled in Miami. They were middle-class, educated people who had worked at good jobs and led comfortable lives in Cuba. Leaving their country meant leaving everything behind. Many became penniless for the first time in their lives.

Miami was overwhelmed by the needs of the refugees flocking to their city. Resentment toward the Spanish-speaking newcomers grew. It was common to see signs on apartments saying, "NO CHILDREN. NO PETS. NO CUBANS."

Many of the Cuban exiles settled in a section of downtown Miami that became known as "Little Havana." Cuban restaurants and businesses lined the streets, and Spanish was spoken everywhere. The people were linked by their common language and experiences—and by their hatred of Fidel Castro. At first, most of them did not see the need to adapt to the American way of life. Like Gloria's mother, they expected Castro to be overthrown quickly, and then they would return home to Cuba. Gloria still has the other half of her $21 round-trip ticket.

The Fajardo family found a tiny, run-down apartment in a Cuban ghetto behind the Orange Bowl Stadium. Gloria's mother put newspapers under the sheets, hoping they would keep away the cockroaches.[5] It was a depressing change from the family's comfortable lifestyle in Havana.

The Cuban refugees and the United States government agreed on one thing: Castro had to go. The Cubans in Miami wanted Castro out of power so they could return home. The United States saw Castro's alliance with the Soviet Union as a threat to U.S. security. Americans who had businesses in Cuba also wanted Castro gone. His Communist government had taken over their businesses and millions of dollars' worth of their property.

The United States Central Intelligence Agency (CIA) came up with a plan to send Cuban exiles on a mission to invade Cuba and overthrow Castro. José Fajardo had

Too Close for Comfort

When Castro formed an alliance with the powerful Soviet Union in 1960, the leaders of the United States were concerned. At that time, the United States and the Soviet Union were locked in the Cold War—a war with no actual battles, but a great deal of fear and distrust. The Soviet presence only ninety miles from Florida threatened America's security. It gave the Soviets access to Cuba's military bases, from which nuclear missiles could be directed at the United States. In 1962, the Soviet Union sent medium-range missiles to Cuba. President John F. Kennedy took a bold stand and demanded that the missiles be removed. The Soviets finally complied, ending the threat of an all-out war. This episode is called the Cuban Missile Crisis.

been in Miami only a short time when he was recruited to join fourteen hundred other exiles willing to take part in the invasion. Their dangerous mission was so secret that when Fajardo left home in August 1960, he could not tell his wife where he was going. He just left her a note saying, "I have to go. You know I can't tell you what I'm doing."[6]

On April 17, 1961, José Fajardo headed up a tank division that landed on the Cuban shore at the Bay of Pigs. The volunteer soldiers had high hopes, but their invasion was doomed from the start. Castro's army was waiting for them. The worn-out American tanks and equipment used by the volunteers were no match for

Castro's forces. Cuban citizens had been expected to join the uprising, but none did. When the United States saw that things were not going well, the government abandoned its support of the plan. The refugee soldiers, including José Fajardo, were left stranded.

The battle in Cuba lasted only one day. Two hundred volunteers were killed. Another twelve hundred were taken prisoner. José Fajardo was captured by his own cousin and imprisoned in Cuba.

Life was a struggle for the families left behind in Miami. "All the men were political prisoners in Cuba, and it was purely women and their kids," Gloria said later. "There was one car the whole community bought for $50, and the one lady that could drive would take everybody to the supermarket and the Laundromat."[7]

Gloria's mother was left to raise her daughter in a strange country under very difficult conditions. She had given up a good life and respected profession to live with poverty and prejudice. She did not speak English and was not able to get a job. Gloria and her mother survived on the small amount of money the United States government gave to families of the volunteers. At the Freedom Tower Refuge Center, Cuban refugees could get surplus food handed out by the Federal government. "We'd get Spam and welfare cheese there because as refugees we couldn't afford anything else. My mother would cover the Spam in Coke to make it brown and sweet," Gloria said.[8]

Even in this depressing setting, music was part of

Even as a little girl, Glorita liked to sing.

Gloria's life. She began singing almost as soon as she started talking. When Gloria was a little older, her mother encouraged her to sing for the women whose husbands were imprisoned in Cuba. Gloria sang songs she had learned from her mother about their Cuban homeland. She was too young to understand why her singing made the homesick women cry.[9]

Gloria was not the only one in the family to show talent at a young age. As a child, Gloria's mother had won a contest in Cuba to be the Spanish-speaking double for child movie star Shirley Temple. She was offered a chance to go to Hollywood to be in a movie, but she never made it into films. Her father refused to let her go.

Late in 1962, President John F. Kennedy gave Cuba $53 million worth of food and medical supplies in return for the release of the so-called Bay of Pigs prisoners. José Fajardo arrived home just in time for Christmas.

Because of his service in Cuba, Fajardo was allowed to join the United States Army as an officer.[10] The family moved to a military base in San Antonio, Texas. Gloria faced a new challenge when she started first grade there. She was the only Spanish-speaking child in her class. Even at that age, Gloria was smart and determined. She quickly tackled the job of learning her new language. Six months later, she won an award for reading well in English.[11]

Gloria was six when her sister Rebecca was born in

Texas. Another member of the family was added later, thanks to Gloria. She loved animals and had always wanted a pet, but the Fajardos' frequent moves made that impossible. When they settled in South Carolina for a couple of years, Gloria begged for a puppy. Her mother finally agreed, but only if Gloria made straight A's in school. Gloria accepted the challenge and got the grades she needed. She chose her pet from a litter of German shepherds. "I knelt down on the ground, and one of the chubby, furry little pups ran right into my arms," she said later. "I picked her up and she started licking my face, and I caught my first whiff of her irresistible puppy breath."[12] Gloria named her puppy Dolly. The dog remained her friend for many years.

During much of the 1960s and early 1970s, the United States was embroiled in a war in Vietnam, a small country in Southeast Asia. In 1966 José Fajardo was sent to Vietnam on an army assignment. "He volunteered for Vietnam, because later on he wanted to go back to the U.S. government and ask them for help to try to go back to Cuba," Gloria said. "So his whole life was very much tied to the whole problem of Cuba."[13]

On Gloria's ninth birthday, her mother surprised her with a guitar. Gloria loved the guitar, but not the rigid classical guitar lessons her mother made her take. Gloria wanted to play the popular songs she listened to on the radio. Johnny Mathis, Barbra Streisand, and Karen Carpenter were three of her favorite singers.

Gloria was thrilled with the guitar she received for her ninth birthday.

Gloria was musical enough to figure out the chords for the songs she loved. She even showed her guitar teacher how to play the popular songs his other students wanted to learn.[14]

Gloria made sure her father did not miss out on her singing while he was in Vietnam. She sang into a tape recorder and sent him the tapes. He wrote back that someday she would be a star.

It was a joyful reunion when Gloria's father returned from Vietnam in 1968. But soon, José Fajardo began acting strange. "He'd fall for no reason," Gloria recalled. "Or he'd stop for a red light, but the light would be green. My mother made him go to the hospital for tests. When he came out, he was already walking with a cane."[15]

The news from the doctors was grim. Gloria's father had multiple sclerosis, or MS. There was no cure for this disease of the nervous system. It would slowly destroy his physical and mental abilities.

The family could not understand how this could happen to a healthy soldier and former athlete. Some people think that his medical condition was triggered by exposure to the chemical mixture Agent Orange while in Vietnam. The military used Agent Orange to strip leaves off trees and brush to make it harder for the enemy to hide. Still, no matter what had caused Fajardo's disease, it was up to the Fajardo family to deal with it.

The burden of supporting the family fell to Gloria's mother. She worked all day, then went to school at night so that she could become certified to teach in Miami. With her mother gone, Gloria had to shoulder many jobs at home. Beginning when she was eleven, Gloria came home from school every day to take care of her father and younger sister, Becky. It was a tremendous amount of responsibility for someone so young. "I was handling a lot, trying to be strong for my mom," Gloria said later.[16]

Gloria's father's physical and mental condition grew worse. "My father would stand up, forget he couldn't walk and fall down," Gloria said. "I had to pick him up a lot, and he felt bad about that."[17] As her father's condition worsened, Gloria had to feed him and even bathe him. It was embarrassing for both of them. Only one thing brought Gloria relief. "When my father was ill, music was my escape," Gloria said. "I would lock myself up in my room for hours and just sing. I wouldn't cry—I refused to cry. . . . Music was the only way I had to just let go, so I sang for fun and for emotional catharsis."[18]

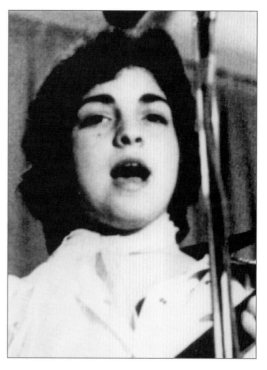

"Music was the one bright spot in my life," said Gloria of her high school years.

Gloria attended the Lourdes Academy, a Catholic girls' school in Miami. She was so serious and introverted that some of the nuns expected her to become a nun herself someday. "She had no life," Becky said. "She took care of Dad and me. She didn't go out; she didn't date. All she would do is sit in her room and play her guitar."[19]

When Gloria was sixteen, her father needed more care than the family could give him. He was sent to a Veterans Administration hospital. At last, Gloria's responsibilities eased. But her life was still painful. Like many teenagers, Gloria was self-conscious and unsure of herself. "When I was a teenager, I was fat, I was shy, I wore glasses, I had a big eyebrow and hair all over my body. They were years of torture. It was very depressing and scary, for me. Music was the one bright spot in my life," Gloria said.[20]

Still, some good came out of Gloria's difficult teen years. The time she spent caring for her father contributed to the kind of person Gloria became. It also increased the importance of music in her life. She was a teenager full of talent, but it would take someone very special to turn her into a star.

3

Prince Charming

Seventeen-year-old Gloria did not want to go to the wedding. The bride was the daughter of her mother's friend. Gloria hardly knew her. She went only so that her mother would not have to attend the wedding alone. It was the summer of 1975.

The reception was a lively affair. Music was provided by a local band, the Miami Latin Boys. The band's leader and keyboardist was Emilio Estefan. It was not the first time Gloria had seen Emilio. A few months earlier he had helped Gloria and some of her friends put together a band for a party. "I'll never forget that he played *The Hustle* on the accordion," Gloria said about their first meeting. "He wore these little shorts, and he was so cute—with great legs."[1]

Emilio recognized Gloria at the wedding. He knew that she could sing and asked her to join the band for a couple of numbers. At first, Gloria refused. She did not like performing in front of strangers. Gloria's mother reminded her that some of the guests were the women Gloria had sung to as a young child. They had not heard her sing in a long time.[2] Gloria finally gave in. She took the microphone and sang a couple of popular Cuban songs. When she finished, the guests stood up and applauded enthusiastically.[3]

The Miami Latin Boys were like dozens of other bands in the area. They spent their weekends playing at weddings, bar mitzvahs, and other special events. At that time, Cuban bands traditionally had only male musicians. Hearing Gloria sing made Emilio consider breaking that tradition. Adding a female singer would set their band apart from the others.

> **Gloria did not want to perform in front of strangers.**

A few days later, Emilio asked Gloria to join the Miami Latin Boys. She turned him down. She was about to start attending the University of Miami on a partial scholarship and did not want anything to interfere with her studies. But Emilio persisted. He convinced Gloria that she could go to school during the week and sing on the weekends. Gloria finally agreed. Emilio also hired Gloria's cousin Merci so that Gloria would not have to be the only woman in the band.

Like Gloria, Emilio had lived in Cuba. His family had moved to Cuba from Lebanon when he was young. His father ran a small clothing factory in Santiago,

Cuba. When Castro's government took control of the factory, Emilio's parents decided it was time to leave the country. But there was a problem. Emilio's older brother, José, was old enough to be drafted into Castro's army. The government would not let José leave. Emilio's parents did not want both their sons to be forced to serve in the Cuban Army. The only solution was for the family to split up. When Emilio was thirteen, he and his father moved to Spain. His mother stayed behind with José.

Life was difficult in Spain. Emilio's father was not able to find work. He and Emilio lived in very poor conditions and ate many of their meals at soup kitchens. Sometimes Emilio played his old accordion in restaurants in return for free food.[4] Finally, when Emilio was fifteen, he was given a student visa, a document allowing him to enter the United States to go to school. He moved into his aunt's crowded house in Miami, where thirteen of his cousins were already staying. Emilio slept on the floor, but at least he was in America. It was another year before his father was allowed to follow him to the United States.

Even as a teenager, Emilio was industrious. To earn money, he bought a beat-up Volkswagen and ran errands for the women in the neighborhood. He bought a better accordion and played at an Italian restaurant where diners gave him tips. Emilio even ran beauty pageants for local girls. He saved money by recycling ribbons from flower arrangements at a funeral home to use as sashes for the contestants.[5] His first full-time job was in the mailroom of Bacardi International, a company that imported rum. It was a hectic life.

"I used to go to Bacardi at seven in the morning, work all day, and then I used to go to school, to finish my night school. Then I used to go to an Italian restaurant every night till twelve or one in the morning to play for tips," Emilio said later.[6]

Emilio's boss at Bacardi knew that Emilio was a musician and hired him to perform at a party he was hosting. Emilio and two friends played for nine hours. After that, Emilio put together the Miami Latin Boys, with Juan Marcos Avila on bass, Kiki Garcia on drums, and Raul Murciano on keyboards and saxophone.

When Gloria and Merci joined the band, the name "Miami Latin Boys" no longer fit. Someone suggested calling it Miami Sound Machine. Gloria did not like the name, but Emilio thought it was catchy.

Being part of the band was a big change for the shy schoolgirl who had done most of her singing alone in her room. Gloria suddenly had a social life. As part of the band, she was going to parties every weekend and getting paid for it.

Gloria admitted that some parts of being in a band were better than others. "What I loved most about the band when I joined was the rehearsals, putting the music together, writing, recording. The performance part was something I did because I had to."[7]

Gloria usually stayed in the background during

performances. Emilio nudged her into singing solos. One night while the band was performing at a hotel, Gloria sang her first solo. She picked a ballad called "What a Difference a Day Makes."

Gloria's college years were busy. During the week, she kept up with her heavy class load. She also worked part-time as an interpreter for the U.S. Customs Service at the Miami airport, where she helped travelers who did not speak English. On weekends she sang with Miami Sound Machine.

One of the reasons Miami Sound Machine was so popular as a party band was that the musicians could play so many different types of music. Gloria was used to singing ballads and hit songs from the radio. Now she added fiery Cuban and South American dance tunes to the mix. She also had to include songs that were favorites of African-American listeners. She became more versatile as a musician.

> *"What I loved most about the band when I joined was the rehearsals, putting the music together, writing, recording."*
> —Gloria Estefan

Gloria was only seventeen when she joined Miami Sound Machine. She liked twenty-three-year-old Emilio from the beginning, but never imagined having a

Gloria began to take center stage as the featured singer in the band.

romantic relationship with him. Emilio flirted with her, but his style was to flirt with everyone. Since his girlfriend at the time was thirty-six, Gloria assumed that Emilio preferred older women. Still, he was fun to work with. Gloria left it at that.

Gloria's sister, Becky, described Emilio as "the catch of the town. Handsome, driving around town in his Corvette, he had rubbed so much leather cleaner into those seats that you'd slide forward every time he hit the brakes!"[8]

From the beginning, Emilio was attracted to Gloria, but he kept his distance.[9] After everything Gloria had been through in her life, Emilio was afraid she would not be able to handle a romantic breakup if that were to happen. Emilio told his mother, "I am not going to make a move on this girl unless I am serious. If she's in love with me and I'm not ready, she will be destroyed."[10]

Even when the attraction grew, neither Gloria nor Emilio wanted to admit it. "We didn't want to jeopardize our working relationship," Gloria said.[11] Finally, Emilio made the first move. Miami Sound Machine was playing at a celebration aboard a ship on July 4, 1976. During a break, Gloria and Emilio went out on the deck to watch fireworks. Emilio asked Gloria for a kiss, saying that it was his birthday. She knew it was not, but finally agreed. Gloria started to kiss him on the cheek, but Emilio turned and kissed her on the lips.[12] After that

The "Miami Sound"

Some of the music popular in Miami became known as the "Miami sound." It was a mixture of rock and pop with a Latin flavor. With so many people of Cuban heritage living in Miami, it is easy to understand the Cuban influence on music there. Cubans had developed a style of music called *son*, which combined the strong rhythms and drums of the African slaves with the melodies of Spanish guitars. When *son* came to Havana in the 1920s, trumpets were added. *Son* evolved into *salsa*, a lively pulsating sound played primarily for dancing. *Salsa* quickly became one of the most popular forms of Latin music and the basis of the "Miami sound."

Watching herself perform on videotape helped Gloria focus her self-improvement plan—with great results.

night, the two finally admitted their true feelings for each other.

In 1977 Miami Sound Machine spent $2,000 to produce its first album, *Renacer (Live Again)*. It contained a mixture of Cuban songs, disco, and ballads. The songs were sung in English on one side of the album and in Spanish on the other. The band went on to produce two more albums cut in both Spanish and English.

Emilio had a playful nature, but when it came to business he admitted to being a perfectionist.[13] His attention to detail even included Gloria's appearance. He once told her that she could improve herself 95 percent. "He was trying to make me confident, but at the time I could've smacked him," Gloria said.[14] She accused him of liking only 5 percent of her. Later, she decided that "Emilio saw a side of me that I didn't let people see, and he wanted that to come out."[15]

Emilio encouraged Gloria to begin dieting and exercising. Her efforts paid off. Her confidence grew, and she lost some of her shyness. "I used to kid him after that: 'Okay, what am I down to? Seventy-five percent? Sixty?'" Gloria laughed.[16] Gloria also took on the challenge of improving her skills as a performer with her usual determination. "It was a painful process, but I forced myself to do it, mostly by watching myself [performing] on videotape, which is the most horrendous experience there is. But it's the only way you can see what other people are seeing," she said.[17]

As the success of Miami Sound Machine grew, so did

the love between Gloria and Emilio. He bought an engagement ring to give Gloria on Valentine's Day in 1978. He was too impatient to wait, though, so he gave her the ring two days early. To make matters worse, he proposed in front of his mother. Gloria was embarrassed at having her future mother-in-law as an audience for her proposal. She later learned that Emilio's mother wanted to see the look on Gloria's face when she got the ring. "Maybe he figured, 'well if my mom is there, she won't say no,'" Gloria joked.[18]

There was not much chance that Emilio would be turned down. Gloria accepted the ring and began preparing for her future.

4

The Machine Starts Rolling

By the time Gloria reached her twenty-first birthday on September 1, 1978, she was already quite accomplished. She had graduated with honors from the University of Miami, finishing all her courses in only three years instead of the usual four. She had majored in both psychology and communications. She was singing in a band that was successful in many countries. And the next day she would marry the love of her life.

There were two unusual things about Gloria and Emilio's wedding. First, the bride broke with tradition and walked down the aisle alone. She would have much preferred to be on the arm of her father. But José Fajardo lay bedridden at the Veterans Hospital. There was no other man in Gloria's life important enough to replace him at that special time.

Although Gloria's father could not attend her wedding, she made sure that he was included in the

Emilio was Gloria's first boyfriend. This photo of the couple was taken in 1990.

happy occasion. After the ceremony, the wedding party visited Fajardo in the hospital. By that time, his disease had affected his mind to the point that he rarely recognized Gloria. As she approached his bed, someone asked him if he knew who she was. Fajardo looked at his daughter in her wedding gown and mouthed a single word—"Glorita." It was only one word, but it was enough to make Gloria and Emilio feel that he was blessing their marriage.[1]

The second unusual thing about Gloria and Emilio's wedding was their reception. They did not have one. This may seem odd for a couple whose business included performing at wedding receptions. But money was tight for the young couple. They preferred to spend it on a honeymoon in Japan.

The next year, Gloria made her first trip back to Cuba since she had left as a toddler. She and Emilio went to help his brother, José. Emilio had tried for fourteen years to get José and his two children out of Cuba. The Cuban government would not let them leave. In 1979, Gloria and Emilio used their connections with the president of Costa Rica to get José and his children visas to travel to Costa Rica.[2] When the Cuban authorities found out, they began pressuring José's family to stay. Life became so difficult that the family was forced to go into hiding. Gloria and Emilio took them clothes and food to help get them through their two months of waiting.

Gloria and Emilio spent a week in Cuba. They shopped at special stores where people with American passports and American dollars could buy food. Everything was extremely expensive. A small can of peaches cost $14. They spent $4,000 on groceries for José's family.

Seeing the way people in Cuba were living upset Gloria. She noticed that when she tried to take a hot shower, only three drops of water would come out. "A mother can't bathe her baby, can't feed it, you know, people are suffering there and that really bothers me," Gloria said.[3]

> "A mother can't bathe her baby, can't feed it, you know, people are suffering there and that really bothers me."
> —Gloria Estefan

More than seven hundred Cuban refugees crowded into this tugboat bound for the United States in 1980.

Two months later, José and his children left for Costa Rica. From there they traveled to the United States.

In 1980, Gloria's father, José Fajardo, died after having battled MS for more than twelve years. But on a happy note, Gloria gave birth to a son on September 2, 1980. He was named Nayib, meaning "good person" in Arabic, the language spoken in Lebanon, where Emilio lived as a young child.

As much as Gloria loved her baby son, she chose not

Life in Cuba

Cuba has more than 11 million people. More than half live in cities. In spite of receiving free education and free medical care, the majority of Cubans are poor. Since the government owns almost all of the land and businesses, nearly everyone works for the government. The average salary is about $10 per month. Housing shortages are common, forcing many people to live in run-down and overcrowded conditions. Very few people in Cuba can afford cars. Citizens are given food rations, but a month's ration may last only a couple of weeks. Rations include very little meat and no fruits and vegetables. Milk is provided only for children up to age seven. To shop, Cubans must stand in long lines at government-run stores whose shelves have almost no variety and may be nearly empty. Traveling to Cuba is forbidden for most United States citizens.

to give up her career to become a full-time mother. "Nine times out of 10, your kids don't appreciate it when you do. And when you give up something of yourself, you're usually not as happy as you were before. And if you're not happy with yourself, it's very difficult to make someone else happy," she said.[4]

Gloria's decision to keep her career did not surprise her family. Both her mother and her grandmother were strong, independent women. They taught Gloria that she could be anything she wanted to be. Gloria's grandmother had kept her independence even into old age. When Gloria's grandfather died, her grandmother learned how to drive and got a driver's license. She was seventy-three at the time.[5]

By the early 1980s, things were going very well for the Estefans. Through several promotions at Bacardi, Emilio had become head of Hispanic marketing. Miami Sound Machine was also gaining success. In 1980, the band signed with Discos CBS International, the Miami-based, Hispanic division of CBS Records. Between 1980 and 1984, Miami Sound Machine released four Spanish-language albums on their new label: *Miami Sound Machine* in 1980; *Otra Vez* (Another Time) in 1981; *Rio* (River) in 1982; and *A Toda Máquina* (At Full Speed) in 1984. As with their first album, these new records contained a mixture of ballads, disco dance tunes, and traditional Latin music. Sales were low in the United States, where they generated interest only in Spanish-speaking communities. But the albums soared to the number-one spot on the album sales charts in several Latin American countries. Miami Sound Machine was used to playing to audiences of a few thousand in the United States. Suddenly, they were playing to thirty thousand or forty thousand people packed into soccer stadiums throughout Latin America.

The first time Gloria had to sing in front of a massive audience was at a festival in Chile, in South America. When Gloria looked out, she could see more than sixty-five thousand people blanketing the hillside. She was so nervous that her knees were knocking. "I always thought that was just an expression. . . . You can actually hear the noise of your knees hitting each other louder than you can hear your heart thumping," Gloria said.[6] She was glad she was wearing a skirt so that no one could see her rattling knees. It did not help that Gloria had heard that crowds often threw things at performers they did not like. She need not have worried. The crowd loved her.

> *Miami Sound Machine was soaring to the top of the charts in Latin America.*

Emilio was torn between his position at Bacardi and the responsibilities of managing the band. Since he was more passionate about the success of Miami Sound Machine, he quit his $100,000-a-year job at Bacardi in 1982.[7] That freed up his time to concentrate on writing songs, producing albums, and taking care of the details of Miami Sound Machine's heavy performance schedule.[8]

Emilio had a clear vision of where he wanted the band to go. He was so focused on the band's success that he did not always consider the effects his decisions had on the other band members. Some of them thought he was favoring Gloria over the other members. For the first eight years she had been part of the team. Now Emilio seemed to be pushing her out in front.[9]

Raul Murciano was one of the discontented band members. He disagreed with the way Emilio divided up the money.[10] After an argument with Emilio, Murciano left the band. His wife, Gloria's cousin Merci, quit the next week.

Throughout the early 1980s, Miami Sound Machine gained in popularity in many countries. They sold a million albums in Europe in 1984, but at home they could not make it onto the American pop chart. This was about to change, thanks to a drummer named Kiki.[11]

5

Crossover!

Enrique "Kiki" Garcia was the popular drummer for Miami Sound Machine. He was so full of energy on stage that his fans nicknamed him the "engine" of the band.[1] Kiki also wrote songs for the band. Usually, he wrote a song in English, then gave it to Gloria to translate into Spanish. One day he wrote a catchy dance tune called "Dr. Beat." It started with a siren to call everyone to the dance floor. This zany song could not be easily translated into Spanish.

The band had been looking for a song to record in English. "Dr. Beat" seemed to be just what they wanted. The producers at Discos CBS International disagreed. Miami Sound Machine had become famous because of their songs in Spanish. The producers did not think their fans would accept a song in English.[2] The band insisted. Finally CBS agreed to put "Dr. Beat" on the

"B" side of a single record, the side for songs not expected to become hits.

While the Spanish-language stations played the "A" side of Miami Sound Machine's new single record, the Anglo stations started giving "Dr. Beat" airtime. Before long, the catchy disco song with the Latin beat could be heard in dance clubs all across the United States. The popularity of "Dr. Beat"crossed the ocean and reached the top of the charts in Europe.

After seeing the success of "Dr. Beat," CBS agreed to switch Miami Sound Machine from Discos CBS International—the Spanish-language division—to Epic Records, the international rock music division of CBS. In 1984 Miami Sound Machine released its first all-English album, *Eyes of Innocence*. It included the popular "Dr. Beat." *Eyes of Innocence* was somewhat successful, but it still was not the breakthrough the band was looking for.

Miami Sound Machine toured Europe to promote *Eyes of Innocence*. Fans in the Netherlands wanted to hear a conga. The conga is a traditional Cuban dance whose name came from the large African drums that give it its beat. The dancers form a long line by holding on to the waist of the person in front of them. Dancers take three steps forward, then kick their foot out to the side on the fourth beat. The bouncing line of dancers snakes around the dance floor or wherever the leader decides to take it.

Kiki Garcia thought about the conga during a flight

between Amsterdam and London. He came up with the words "C'mon, shake your body, baby, do the conga / I know you can't control yourself any longer." His song, simply named "Conga," took off from there.

When CBS executives heard "Conga," they were certain that it would never be played on Anglo radio.[3] "This producer told us that the song was 'too Latin for the Americans, and too American for the Latins'. I said 'thank you, that's exactly what we are! We're a mix,'" Gloria Estefan said.[4]

This Estefan single features "Don't Wanna Lose You" on one side and "Si Voy a Perderte"—the same song in Spanish—on the other.

The producers finally allowed "Conga" to be released as a single.

Miami Sound Machine hoped that "Conga" would become a crossover hit. To be classified as a hit, a song must be high on the chart—the list of hits compiled by groups such as *Billboard* magazine. *Billboard* has several charts to reflect the different types of music people enjoy. There are charts for pop, black, Latin, country western, dance, rock, etc. If a song gets on two or more charts, it is called a "crossover" hit. Not many songs reach crossover status. It is difficult to find a song that appeals to more than one type of listener.

"Conga" was more than a crossover hit. It was a crossover explosion. It broke all records by becoming the first song in history to be on four music charts at the same time. It appeared on *Billboard*'s Latin, black, dance, and pop charts. The record still stands. "Conga" also gave Miami Sound Machine its first gold record by selling more than 500,000 copies.

Encouraged by the success of "Conga," Miami

"C'mon . . . do the conga": With "Conga," Miami Sound Machine had its first crossover hit.

Music Charts

Each week, *Billboard*, a music industry magazine, publishes a variety of charts to rank the week's most popular songs and albums. They also put out their "Hot 100" chart to rank the top 100 pop songs. The "Top 40" hits come from this chart. A song's chances of making it onto a chart are determined by two things—airplay and sales. The most important factor is airplay, or how often a song is played on the radio or music video channels on TV. Modern technology is used to recognize the digital patterns in songs. This allows each song to be counted every time it is played on radio or TV. More than a million songs are counted each year. Sales are counted by collecting the data obtained when bar codes are scanned at the cash register during a purchase.[5]

Sound Machine was ready to put together another album in English. Emilio wanted the band to have a unique sound. He was impressed with three musicians who called themselves the Jerks. Emilio first heard Joseph Galdo, Rafael Vigil, and Lawrence Dermer when they were recording a song for an aerobic exercise project called *Salsa-cize*. Emilio hired the Jerks to help with the next album, *Primitive Love*.

Epic was willing to spend $20,000 to produce *Primitive Love*. Emilio and Gloria wanted more. They were so confident that the album would be successful that they invested their entire life savings of $32,000 in the project.[6] The gamble paid off. Listeners in the United States were captivated by the new sound blending pop with Latin rhythms and instruments. *Primitive Love* sold 1.5 million copies in the United States and 4 million copies worldwide. Three of the songs—"Conga," "Words Get in the Way," and "Bad Boys"—all became Top 10 hit singles in the United States.

Gloria wrote two of the hit songs for *Primitive Love.* "Bad Boys" was a lively dance tune, while "Words Get in the Way" was her first hit ballad. Gloria wrote "Words Get in the Way" after an argument with Emilio. During their disagreement, Gloria could not find the right words to express how she felt. She took that frustration and turned it into a song. It was the first time many listeners had heard Gloria's rich sultry voice. She was compared to the late Karen Carpenter, a singer who was popular in the 1970s. That was a compliment for Gloria, who had spend many hours as a teenager singing along to Karen Carpenter's romantic ballads on the radio.

On *Primitive Love*, ballads were mixed in with the Latin dance numbers and lively pop songs. It proved that Miami Sound Machine was more than just a Latin band that specialized in gimmicky Latin dance tunes. Gloria was pleased with the change. "Ballads are basically what I'm about. I just feel you can express yourself more completely and eloquently in a ballad. It's easier to identify with someone else and form a bond with the audience," she explained.[7]

There was an important change on the album cover for *Primitive Love*. Only Gloria's picture appeared on the front. The other members of the band were pictured on the back. The Jerks were not pictured at all. "You need a magnifying glass to see our credits," Galdo complained.[8] He felt that the Jerks' work in writing, arranging, and performing on the album gave Miami Sound Machine its distinctive Latin/pop sound. "All you have to do is go and buy the albums they did before *Primitive Love* and compare them. It's the difference between night and day," Galdo said.[9] This issue of recognition for the musicians' role would lead to friction between the Jerks and Emilio Estefan.

Gloria Estefan and Miami Sound Machine went on a world tour to promote *Primitive Love*. They put on more than one hundred concerts in the United States, Central America, Europe, and Japan. Not all the places they visited were safe. At that time, the Central American country of El Salvador was in the midst of a violent civil war. Special steps were taken to ensure the safety of the band members. Estefan was protected by three bodyguards

> *"Ballads are basically what I'm about. I just feel you can express yourself more completely and eloquently in a ballad."*
>
> **—Gloria Estefan**

carrying Uzi submachine guns.[10] As Miami Sound Machine took the stage before forty thousand fans, a series of explosions cracked the air. The band members dropped to the floor to avoid being hit by gunfire. When they looked up they saw colorful fireworks filling the sky to welcome them. Everyone laughed as the band members got back on their feet and continued the concert.[11]

The popularity of Miami Sound Machine extended beyond Spanish- and English-speaking countries. In 1986 the band won first prize at the Tokyo Music Festival. Before performing, the band members were warned that Japanese audiences were very reserved and were unlikely to offer more than polite applause. "Then after the first song, they all jumped out of their seats and were dancing for the whole show," Estefan said.[12]

Emilio stopped performing with the band in 1987, after *Primitive Love*. Miami Sound Machine was now a big business. Emilio wanted to devote more time to producing the band's albums and managing his wife's career. He also wanted to begin producing albums for other singers.

The success of Gloria and Miami Sound Machine made them popular with companies who wanted her to advertise their products. Gloria was careful about the products she would endorse. She and Emilio had a good reputation and were considered good role models. They did not drink or do drugs. They were known for their strong, faithful marriage and were devoted parents

Miami Sound Machine won the grand prize at the Tokyo Music Festival in 1986, where their Japanese fans danced with enthusiasm.

to their son, Nayib. No matter how much money was offered, Gloria would not promote anything that would tarnish the Estefans' image or that of the band.

Gloria accepted the opportunity to perform in a worldwide Pepsi commercial in both English and Spanish. But in 1985 she turned down an invitation to appear on the popular television drama *Miami Vice*. The script called for the band to be playing at a party during a drug bust. It was not the image Gloria wanted for herself or her city. "*Miami Vice* has conjured up images of drugs and violence, we're goodwill ambassadors for the city," Gloria said.[13]

Likewise, the City of Miami preferred to focus on its

more positive aspects. One of those was the success of Gloria and Miami Sound Machine. City officials presented the band with a key to the city. They even changed the name of the street where the Estefans lived to Miami Sound Machine Boulevard.

Gloria and Miami Sound Machine ended 1986 on a high note. At the American Music Awards, they won awards for the Best New Pop Artists and Top Pop Singles Artists. They recorded "Hot Summer Nights" for the movie *Top Gun*, starring Tom Cruise. Gloria and Kiki wrote the song "Suave" for the movie *Cobra*, starring Sylvester Stallone. But Gloria was about to learn that success could have a downside, too. It was about to separate her from the people she loved the most.

6

Letting It Loose

Primitive Love had brought Gloria Estefan and Miami Sound Machine to the attention of the English-speaking American public. It was their next album, *Let It Loose*, released in 1987, that secured their fame. Four of the album's songs became Top 10 hits, including "1-2-3," "Rhythm Is Gonna Get You," "Anything for You," and "I Can't Stay Away from You." *Let It Loose* reached the top of the album charts in Europe, Australia, and Canada. It sold nearly 8 million copies around the world and stayed on the charts for more than two years.

While *Let It Loose* was still in the planning stages, Epic Records was busy revising its marketing strategy for Miami Sound Machine. The record company began to focus even more on Gloria Estefan. Tommy Mottola, president of CBS Records—Epic's parent company— recognized her potential. "When you have a mass appeal artist with a strong Latin base who writes and sings her own songs, there's no limit to what you can do and how long you can do it," he said.[1] The new focus included changing the name of the band from Miami Sound Machine to Gloria Estefan and Miami Sound Machine.

By that time, music videos were an important marketing tool for recording artists. Estefan had made music videos before, but they did not measure up to those being shown on the cable television channels MTV and VH-1. CBS Records brought in experts to spice up Estefan's videos to make them more competitive. This included updating her appearance.

Estefan went through a complete makeover, with changes to her wardrobe and her makeup. She let her hair grow long and curled it into soft ringlets. Estefan also began a fitness program. She hired a personal trainer and worked out regularly. Eventually she was doing six hundred sit-ups and running four miles a day. The effort paid off. The five-foot-two-inch beauty trimmed down and firmed up.

Estefan put a lot of effort into improving herself beyond her appearance, too. "There's no growth without a lot of hard work and a little risk," she has said. "It's important to me that I continue to grow. There's no point in living life any other way."[2]

Estefan was already respected as a gifted singer and energetic performer. On *Let It Loose*, her talent as a songwriter became even more evident.

Normally, Estefan spent weeks or even months writing a song. She wanted every detail to be perfect.

Estefan worked hard to be in tip-top shape for her music videos.

But her hit "Anything for You" was written in one sitting over a cup of coffee at a hamburger shop. Estefan recorded the song that same day in only one take. Then three days before the band had to turn in the master tapes, Gloria decided the song was not exactly right. The band spent the next three days and nights re-recording the music behind Gloria's vocals. "We didn't sleep for three straight days," Emilio recalled. "Talk about exhaustion!"[3] But it was worth the effort. "Anything for You" became Gloria's first number-one hit.

Estefan tried to keep politics out of her music, but she sometimes got drawn into controversy without even trying.

In 1987, Miami Sound Machine was invited to perform at the closing ceremonies of the Pan-American Games in Indianapolis, Indiana. The Pan-American Games are held every four years, with competing athletes from the countries of the Americans. This athletic competition had special meaning for Gloria. In 1952 her father had won a bronze medal at the games as part of Cuba's volleyball team. Gloria still has his medal.

The delegation from Cuba was outraged that a band headed by Cuban exiles had been invited to perform. They threatened to boycott the closing ceremonies if Miami Sound Machine appeared. Estefan did not back down. "We are going to be present there," she insisted. "We are going to demonstrate what freedom really means, carrying a message of freedom not only to Cubans, but also to Latin America."[4]

Gloria and Miami Sound Machine played to the crowd of more than forty thousand people at the closing ceremonies. The Cuban athletes attended, but while the rest of the audience danced and cheered, the athletes from Cuba sat silently in protest.[5]

Near the end of 1987, Miami Sound Machine went on a world tour to promote *Let It Loose*. At that time, Nayib was six years old. Little League baseball was more important to him than traipsing around the world with his parents. Gloria did not want to disrupt her son's life any more than necessary. She also felt it was important for Nayib to have at least one parent with him. The only solution was for Gloria to go on tour while Emilio stayed home with Nayib.

The *Let It Loose* tour was grueling. "We travel on a bus with twelve bunks," Estefan said. "After a hard night of performing and partying, we end up sleeping in our little 'coffins' during the day . . . just like Dracula."[6] In spite of the exhausting schedule, Estefan always had to be energetic for the next performance. Her fans expected it.

The *Let It Loose* tour ended with a triumphant homecoming. Two concerts were performed before standing-room-only crowds in the Miami Arena. Videotapes of the concerts were edited together and

Long Live "Conga"!

With the popularity of Miami Sound Machine's song "Conga," competitions sprang up to see who could put together the longest conga line. For a while, Burlington, Vermont, held the record for its line of nearly eleven thousand dancers. In 1988 Gloria and Miami Sound Machine helped shatter that record at Miami's annual Calle Ocho (Eighth Street) Festival in Little Havana. As Estefan stood on a stage set up on the roof of a bank building, she belted out "Conga" over loudspeakers. Nearly 120,000 people formed a conga line below her. The line of dancers three miles long stepped and kicked their way down *Calle Ocho*. The *Guinness Book of Records* declared the Calle Ocho conga line the longest one in the world. The record still stands.[7]

Estefan displayed the American Music Award that she and the band won on January 30, 1989.

broadcast on the Showtime cable channel. It went on to win three Cable Ace Awards for Best Music Special, Best Directing, and Best Editing.

As Gloria Estefan and Miami Sound Machine became more successful, they began receiving awards from organizations within the music industry. In 1989, Miami Sound Machine won the American Music Award as the best pop/rock band of the year. The same year, Gloria won the American Billboard Award for Songwriter of the Year. Emilio and the Jerks were nominated for a Grammy that year as Producers of the Year for *Let It Loose*, but they did not win.

In spite of two successful albums, the relationship between Emilio and the Jerks continued to be strained. The Jerks felt that they deserved more recognition and money for their work on *Primitive Love* and *Let It Loose*. The situation worsened when Emilio tried to sign the Jerks to an exclusive contract. "He wanted to sign us to a five-year deal that was very one-sided," Galdo said.[8] When they could not come to an agreement with Emilio, the Jerks left the band.

Although Galdo had problems with Emilio, he was impressed with Gloria. He described her as being "naturally musical and a real hard worker. No prima donna groove. If there was something wrong with a track at four in the morning, she'd say, 'Okay, let's work on it.'"[9]

The Jerks were not the only ones to leave. Another blow came at the end of the *Let It Loose* tour when Kiki Garcia left the band. Garcia's departure left Gloria as the only remaining member of the original Miami Sound Machine. Emilio filled out the band by hiring musicians from the University of Miami music department.

Emilio was a sharp businessman with a strong drive for success. Some of this drive came from knowing what it was like to lose everything. "It's the immigrant mentality," Gloria explained. "Both our families were very well off in Cuba. Then all of a sudden, boom, you're here. You have nothing. It's hard to get rid of that feeling."[10]

Gloria's talents as a singer and songwriter, combined with Emilio's skills and drive as a businessman, brought the couple sizable wealth. They bought a multimillion-dollar home on exclusive Star Island in Miami. Gloria could look across the water from their five-bedroom, two-story home and see the Miami skyline. She had come a long way from her first Miami home in a tiny roach-infested apartment behind the Orange Bowl.

Although Estefan had become a pop star in the United States, she did not want to ignore the Spanish-speaking fans who had stuck by her from the beginning of her career. Her next album, *Cuts Both Ways*, embraced both groups. Even the title, *Cuts Both Ways*, is a play on words. In the recording industry, a "cut" is one song on an album. On this album, there were cuts—or songs—in both English and Spanish.

Gloria wrote seven of the ten songs on *Cuts Both Ways*. Her importance to the album was also obvious on

By 1989, Gloria was being featured as a solo vocalist with Miami Sound Machine as her backup band.

the record jacket. The name *Gloria Estefan* stood alone. Miami Sound Machine was mentioned only on the back cover. It was a clear sign that Gloria had graduated to the status of solo pop female vocalist.

The first hit single off *Cuts Both Ways* was the ballad "Don't Wanna Lose You." The song was released in Spanish and English at the same time. It soared to number one on both the American and Latin *Billboard* charts at the same time. It also reached the top of the charts in Norway, Holland, Finland, England, and Japan. For her efforts, Broadcast Music, Inc., a worldwide agency that sells rights to music, honored Estefan with the 1989 Songwriter of the Year Award.

One of the songs Estefan wrote in Spanish was "Oye Mi Canto" (Hear My Song). It was a plea for people to break down racial barriers and reduce prejudice. The video for "Oye Mi Canto" won an international MTV award. But the song entangled Estefan in a lawsuit.

Popular salsa singer and musician Eddie Palmieri, a five-time Grammy winner, claimed that Gloria had stolen the music from his song "Paginas de Mujer." It was one he had written and recorded ten years earlier. He filed a $10-million lawsuit against Gloria Estefan and Sony Music Entertainment (which had acquired CBS Records by then) for copyright violation. Gloria was upset by the charges of stealing music. She insisted that her song did not copy Palmieri's song, but rather was based on the folk melodies she listened to growing up. Palmieri was not able to prove that Gloria had ever heard his song. He lost the lawsuit.

Gloria went on a nine-month worldwide tour to promote *Cuts Both Ways*. This time the entire family went with her. After performing to sold out crowds in Europe, the group came back to the United States to finish the tour. The strain of touring had taken a toll on Gloria's health. She suffered from a cold and influenza, but she was determined not to disappoint her fans. She kept performing until she could no longer sing. A throat specialist determined that her constant coughing had damaged blood vessels in her throat. If Estefan did not give up singing for six months, she would risk permanent damage to her vocal chords. She was not even allowed to talk for two weeks. Estefan canceled several performances and went home to recover. "I was really scared," she admitted. "This is my *life*."[11]

By early 1990, Estefan's voice was as strong as ever. She resumed her tour and began to make up her canceled concerts. She took time out to host the American Music Awards in January. When the Grammy nominations were announced, Gloria learned that she had been nominated for Best Female Vocal Performer, and Emilio had been nominated as Producer of the Year. However, neither of them won.

> **"I was really scared. This is my life."**
> —**Gloria Estefan**

Estefan never took her success for granted. She enjoyed using her celebrity status to make a difference in other people's lives. One of her projects was a campaign designed to keep young people off drugs. Billboards all over the country displayed her picture with the slogan "If you need someone, call a friend. Don't do drugs."[12] The campaign earned Estefan and her family a visit with President George H. W. Bush at the White House in March 1990. It was a wonderful experience that her family would always remember. It was followed by a day that would change Gloria Estefan's life forever.

Coming Out of the Dark

The day after her visit with George H. W. Bush, Gloria was involved in the bus accident that broke her back. Two weeks after the surgery to repair the broken vertebra in her back, she was allowed to go home.

Estefan flew fifteen hundred miles back to her home in Miami in a private plane belonging to a friend, the Spanish singer Julio Iglesias. Long before the plane landed, a crowd of well-wishers, family members, and reporters gathered at the airport. A hush fell over the crowd as the plane landed. When the door of the plane opened and Gloria appeared, the crowd erupted into cheers. Gloria walked cautiously down the steps, hanging on to Emilio for support. Then she sank into the wheelchair waiting for her at the bottom of the steps. Nayib ran up to greet his mother, wearing a sling on his arm to protect his collarbone broken in the accident.

Gloria was wheeled to a podium that had been set up

on the runway. In spite of her pain, she stood up and addressed the crowd. She thanked everyone for their prayers. Then, with her typical sense of humor, she thanked Emilio for "waiting to faint until I got to the hospital." She also thanked Nayib, "who held my hand while we waited for the ambulances and took very good care of me."[1]

Back at home, Gloria began her painful recovery. At first she was completely dependent on Emilio for everything. She could not even wash her face or brush her teeth by herself. At night, Emilio got up with her every forty-five minutes for a walk out to the pier and back to relieve her pain and stiffness. "She used to walk and cry at the same time," Emilio said later. "It was very tough."[2]

For three months, Emilio stayed home from the office to take care of Gloria. "I joke to keep her spirits up. . . . But her suffering kills me inside," Emilio said.[3] He did whatever he could to cheer her up. His therapy included giving Gloria two Dalmatian puppies that had been born the

Nayib was happy to welcome his mom to the Miami airport after her back surgery.

day of her surgery. They named the puppies Ricky and Lucy after the characters in the classic television comedy series *I Love Lucy*.

All through her life, Estefan had been goal-oriented. When a challenge was put before her, she worked hard to achieve it. She attacked her recovery with that same determination.

Progress came slowly. Asked when she finally believed that she would recover, Estefan laughed: "The day I put on my underwear without help. Boy, that was something to celebrate! Then it was small goals each day: walking to the front door, to the gate."[4]

Estefan's personal trainer, Carmen Klepper, understood how difficult it was for Estefan to deal with her injuries. "Imagine someone in great shape who suddenly

The Long Road to Rehabilitation

To reach her goal of performing again, Estefan began her long and difficult struggle to recover. She endured six hours of physical therapy three days a week for a year. She began slowly by swimming and riding a stationary bicycle to strengthen her arm and leg muscles without straining her back. Gradually, under the watchful eye of her physical trainer, she began lifting weights. Eventually she added aerobics to build up the stamina she would need for her performances. She built up strong abdominal muscles to support her back. Even though she recovered many years ago, Estefan still works out regularly to keep her back in shape.

cannot walk," Klepper said. "Mentally, that can crush you. Your body crumbles. But Gloria is recuperating faster than anyone. She has drive like I have never seen."[5]

Estefan improved physically, but she was still hesitant to get back to her music. She was not sure how the accident had affected her voice, so she did not sing for three months. She also suffered from writer's block. Emilio lured Gloria back into writing by telling her about the ray of sunlight that filled the helicopter when they were flying to the hospital in New York. Then he played a little bit of a song he had started.

"Emilio played the lyric, 'coming out of the dark' and I sat down, and it was so easy," Gloria said. "Everything just tumbled out. We finished that song right there. I tried singing that day too. After that, I was in writing mode."[6]

Because of the millions of dollars Gloria had lost due to her injuries, the Estefans filed a lawsuit against everyone they believed to be responsible for the accident. That included the truck driver who hit the bus, the trucking company he worked for, the owner of the shipping containers loaded onto the truck, and even the driver of the skidding truck that had started the chain reaction resulting in the accident. The driver of the truck that hit the Estefans' bus testified that when he applied his brakes, nothing happened. He tried to keep from hitting other drivers, but could not control the runaway truck. The Estefans were awarded $8.3 million in the settlement. They donated some money to the

Ronald McDonald House in Scranton, where Emilio and Nayib had stayed immediately after the accident.

By January 1991, Estefan was ready for her first live public appearance. She performed for the American Music Awards. Estefan was nervous: "Oh, God, my knees were knocking. My heart started beating so hard, I thought it was going to come out of my chest. Then it went down to my knees and I thought, 'Oh no, I won't be able to walk, and people will think it's because of the accident.'"[7] But once Estefan started singing, her nervousness disappeared and she stopped shaking. The audience gave her a standing ovation.

Estefan's biggest test came the night of March 1, 1991. More than twelve thousand fans packed the Miami Arena for the first performance of Estefan's *Into the Light* world tour. It was a very emotional night for Estefan.

As the lights dimmed and the music pulsated through the arena, five dancers jumped and swirled around the stage. One by one they removed the headpieces that matched their blue-sequined jumpsuits. The last dancer was hoisted onto the shoulders of the others. She took off her hood and shook her head to send her dark curls tumbling over her shoulders. The crowd went wild when they realized it was Gloria. She immediately went into an energetic performance of "Get on Your Feet," complete with jumps and vigorous dance steps. It was obvious to everyone: Gloria Estefan was back!

Less than a year after her accident, Estefan triumphantly kicked off her *Into the Light* world tour.

An American Head and a Cuban Heart

Into the Light was an exhausting tour for Estefan. It seemed that all her fans wanted to see for themselves that she had truly recovered from her accident. Her vigorous schedule took her to nine countries on five continents. More than 5 million people listened to her sultry voice and watched the dance moves they thought they would never see her perform again. It came as no surprise that her uplifting song "Coming Out of the Dark" hit number one on the pop music chart.

Estefan was known around the world as a talented singer and songwriter. Less known was her success as a businesswoman. Gloria and Emilio were more than husband and wife. They were also business partners. Together they formed Estefan Enterprises, with Emilio as president and Gloria as vice president. "It is a true partnership," Emilio said. "Anything I do I talk to

Gloria, because she is a smart businessperson and she has the right principles."[1]

In 1991, Estefan Enterprises bought Crescent Moon Recording Studios in Miami. Crescent Moon remains popular among recording artists because of its state-of-the-art technology. The next year Estefan Enterprises bought the historic Cardozo Hotel in the trendy South Beach section of Miami Beach. They also bought a Cuban restaurant, Larios on the Beach, in the same area. Emilio admits that it was Gloria's idea to venture outside the music business. "She said, 'We have the best beaches in the world, the best hotels in the world, and it would be great to say, We made money and the city has been so great to us, so we're putting money back into the city.'"[2]

Estefan began 1992 as a featured performer at the half-time show for football's Super Bowl. It was a chance to show the size of her talent. An incident later that year showed the size of her heart.

In late August 1992, Florida's Atlantic Coast was being threatened by a monster. Hurricane Andrew, one of the most intense storms of the century, was roaring straight toward Florida. Gloria and her family and pets left their home on Star Island and took shelter in their recording studio in Miami. During the night, Hurricane Andrew slammed into south Florida with violent winds clocked as high as 164 miles an hour.

The Estefans waited through the night as the storm raged around them. Occasionally they peeked out through the lobby, but Andrew's terrible roar frightened them back inside.[3] "At one point at about three in the morning, the whole building got sucked to one side," Gloria said. "I was lying on the couch and my back got plastered to the couch. I thought, here we go."[4]

The next morning, Gloria got her first look at Andrew's devastation. It brought tears to her eyes. "It was almost like they dropped the bomb, what I imagine people feel like in a war-torn city," she said.[5]

The Estefans were lucky. They were not hurt by the storm. Even their home on Star Island had been spared.

After Hurricane Andrew devastated parts of Florida, the Estefans immediately pitched in to help.

It was the area south of Miami that received the brunt of Andrew's fury. The violent storm cut a path of destruction one hundred miles long and fifty miles wide. More than three hundred thousand people were left homeless.

Estefan had learned an important lesson during her own tragedy, and she was ready to pass it on to the hurricane victims. "You can't sit there and wallow. You weep for what's gone and then you move ahead."[6] With that, she rolled up her sleeves and got to work. She started by writing a $100,000 check to the United Way's hurricane

Visiting the Victims

In 1992, Estefan spent her birthday handing out food to hurricane victims living in temporary shelters. "It was the best birthday in my life," Estefan said.[7] She also visited the tent city set up at Homestead Air Force Base for homeless victims. Army general Colin Powell later recalled seeing Estefan among the volunteers. She did not look or act like a superstar. She was just another hard-working volunteer showing her concern for others. "She was determined not only to give back in a big way with [her] talent, but to give back also in a small and just as important a way by handing out food to someone in need," Powell said.[8]

relief fund. Then she and Emilio set up a relief center in their office. From there, they collected and distributed clothing to hurricane victims. Gloria even helped rescue some dogs that had been displaced by the storm.[9] She visited people living in temporary shelters whose homes had been destroyed by the storm.

Building up the morale of the victims was good, but it would take money, and lots of it, to help them rebuild their lives. For their most ambitious project, Gloria and Emilio organized a benefit concert. Jimmy Buffett; Whoopi Goldberg; Paul Simon; Crosby, Stills & Nash; Ziggy Marley; Rosie O'Donnell; and the Bee Gees were just a few of the performers who agreed to help.

The night of September 26, 1992, more than fifty-three thousand people packed Joe Robbie Stadium in Miami. There were so many performers that it was nearly 3 A.M. before the last one was done. The concert raised $3 million for the hurricane relief fund.

Gloria still had more to give. A song she had recently written, "Always Tomorrow," became the unofficial theme song of the relief effort. Gloria made a video of the song, showing the devastation caused by Andrew. The proceeds went to the hurricane relief fund. She included an address where people could send donations to help the people who had lost so much in the storm.

The hard work and generosity shown by Gloria and Emilio came as no surprise to the citizens of Miami. They were used to seeing the Estefans helping out. "As immigrants, we have to give back to the community that opened its arms to us and to the land that welcomed us," said Emilio. "People here treat us like family. They see us in the street and come up to offer hugs and kisses."[10]

Even President George H. W. Bush recognized Estefan's desire to help others. In September 1992, he appointed her as a public delegate to the United Nations. It was an honor that Estefan took very seriously. She spent three months working with the Third Committee on Human Rights.

Part of Estefan's job was to give speeches written by the political staff, which presented the United States' position on various issues. She delivered a speech asking the United Nations to budget more money to help refugees around the world, especially those in Africa.[11] Two days later, Estefan was able to express her own opinions to a special committee discussing freedom of information. Estefan spoke out against governments that would not allow the Voice of America radio programs to broadcast pro-democracy views. Speaking in Spanish, Estefan said that no government should censor or control freedom of expression. Although she never mentioned Cuba by name, it was obvious that she was including the country of her birth in her criticism.[12]

Estefan's activities kept up at a rapid pace. In 1992 she released her *Greatest Hits* album. It went platinum, meaning that it sold more than a million copies. She also continued to accumulate awards and honors.

In 1993, Estefan was awarded a star on the famous Hollywood Walk of Fame, and was given an honorary doctor of music degree from the University of Miami. That same year, she was invited to Ellis Island to receive the Ellis Island Congressional Medal of Honor. It is the highest honor awarded to a citizen who was born outside the United States. Estefan even had her likeness sculpted in wax for the "Rock Circus" exhibition in Madame Tussaud's wax museum in London, England.

With their close marriage and close working relationship, it is not surprising that many awards were given to Gloria and Emilio together. In 1993, the Estefans were presented with the Hispanic Heritage Award, which honors Hispanic Americans for their outstanding achievements and their influence as role models to inspire youth. The same year, the United Way in Miami awarded Gloria and Emilio the Alexis de Tocqueville Award for Outstanding Philanthropy for their many contributions to South Florida, especially after Hurricane Andrew.

Estefan is serious about her music and about helping others, but those around her know that she also has a playful sense of humor. She enjoys writing parodies of her songs. She turned "Anything for You" into "Anything for Food." "Coming Out of the Dark" became "I Got Mugged in the Park." Some of her lyrics are a little on the naughty side. "I have to keep my raunchy lyrics to myself," she laughs, adding with a wink, "Everyone has to have a secret side."[13]

Estefan had achieved the success she wanted with her albums in English. Now she was ready to return musically to her Cuban roots. The result was the album *Mi Tierra* (My Homeland). The Spanish songs were new, but were written in the style of music popular in Cuba in the 1930s and 1940s. It was the type of music that could be heard in the nightclubs of Havana before Castro came to power.

Putting out an album in Spanish was risky now

In 1993 Estefan was honored with a star on the Hollywood Walk of Fame.

that Estefan had crossed over to the American mainstream. But it was a project Estefan was passionate about, and her passion showed in her music.

"A lot of people told me at the beginning, 'You're too Latin for the Americans, too American for the Latins,'" she said. "And I say, 'But that's who I am.' I'm Cuban American; I'm not one thing or the other. I have an American head and a Cuban heart."[14]

Mi Tierra was a stunning success. It became the first Spanish-language album to ever earn a gold record in

"I have an American head and a Cuban heart," said Estefan.

the United States by selling more than half a million copies. Worldwide sales topped 5 million. In Spain, *Mi Tierra* became the best-selling album in the country's history. At home, it earned Gloria her first Grammy, in 1994, for the Best Tropical Album.

Thanks to Gloria and others, Latin music was hot. In 1994 the genre earned its own awards show—the Latin Music Awards. The first year, Gloria won more awards than anyone else. *Mi Tierra* won as album of the year in the tropical/salsa category. "Mi Tierra" was named the song of the year, and Gloria won as artist of the year. Emilio won the El Premio Billboard award for his over-all contribution to the Latino music industry.[15]

All the awards in the world could not help Gloria and Emilio with what they were most anxious to produce. Before Gloria's fateful accident, she had planned to take time off at the end of her *Cuts Both Ways* tour to have a second child. After the accident, doctors said her injured back was not strong enough to handle a pregnancy. Estefan worked tirelessly to recover from her broken back only to discover another problem. She would not be able to conceive a child because of damage caused by the accident. Surgery repaired the problem, and within a month Gloria was delighted to discover that a baby was on the way.

Estefan did not let pregnancy slow her down. She recorded *Hold Me, Thrill Me, Kiss Me*, a collection of the old favorites she had grown up with. When it came time to film the video for "Everlasting Love," Estefan was too pregnant to appear on camera. She found five look-alikes and dressed them in outfits she had worn in earlier videos. Typical of Gloria's sense of humor, four of the look-alikes were actually men. Old clips of Gloria were scattered through the video. It became a game for viewers to guess which figures were Gloria and which were stand-ins.

It was a joyous occasion when Emily Marie Estefan was born on December 5, 1994. Emilio stayed in the delivery room and held Gloria's hand for support. "But when they said 'The baby's coming!' he suddenly let go of my hand. I looked at him and he was green. They tell me he was actually the color of the surgical clothes," Gloria reported.[16] Emilio was taken out of the delivery room in a wheelchair. He returned in time to cut the umbilical cord.

Gloria stepped back from her career for a while to devote time to Emily and Nayib. But there was one performance too important to turn down. In 1995, she was invited to perform at the Vatican in Rome, Italy, to celebrate Pope John Paul II's fifty years in the priesthood. Her audience was made up mostly of cardinals, bishops, nuns, priests, and the pope himself. "And I'm thinking to myself, how did I get here?" Estefan recalled. "It was a big honor to be invited to the Vatican, but I didn't know the pope followed my career."[17]

Estefan had always insisted that she would never perform in Cuba as long as Castro was in power. She made an exception in September 1995. At that time there were thousands of Cuban refugees at the U.S. Naval Base at Guantanamo Bay. They were living in tent cities while waiting for permission to move to the United States. Estefan agreed to perform for them to boost their morale.

Gloria and Emilio flew to Guantanamo for a one-day visit. That night, the open-air stage came alive as Gloria performed in both English and Spanish. She sang songs from *Mi Tierra*, celebrating her own Cuban heritage. She also sang songs from her new album *Abriendo Puertas* (Open Doors), which was being released the next day. When she belted out "Conga," the refugees and American soldiers joined together in a huge conga line that snaked through the crowd. After the upbeat occasion, Emilio told Gloria, "If your father had been alive tonight, what a special night it would be for him."[18]

> "*If your father had been alive tonight, what a special night it would be for him.*"
> —Emilio Estefan

Gloria left Guantanamo knowing that she had lifted the spirits of the refugees. Her life was going well. She had a new baby and a string of new awards. *Abriendo Puertas* had just been released. But just when things were going so well, the Estefans were about to be involved in another tragedy.

Reaching Higher

The end of September 1995 was a hectic time for Estefan. She had been giving interviews almost nonstop to promote *Abriendo Puertas*. She had also made the quick trip to Guantanamo to perform for the Cuban refugees there. Finally, on September 24, she and Emilio had some free time. They both loved boating and decided to spend the afternoon on the water.

The beautiful Sunday afternoon had brought many people out to enjoy the sparkling Biscayne Bay. Speedboats and sailboats cruised across the bay. Personal watercraft (such as Jet Skis, Wet Bikes, and WaveRunners) darted between them like motorcycles on water. Some of the riders cut across the wakes left by passing boats. Hitting a wake just right sent them flying through the air for a quick but dangerous thrill.

One of these little vehicles scooting across the water was driven by Maynard Clark, a twenty-nine-year-old law student from Washington, D.C. His girlfriend, Trish Green, was riding on the back.

After going out into the Atlantic Ocean for a while, the Estefans headed back home in their boat. Emilio looked across the water and saw Clark's watercraft speeding toward them. "I think he's going to jump the wake," Emilio told Gloria.[1]

Clark's watercraft cut in front of the Estefans' boat. Suddenly, it turned and crashed into the side of the boat. Clark and Green were hurled into the water by the impact. Green was thrown away from the boat and suffered only minor injuries. Clark was not so lucky. He fell into the path of the boat's twin engines. The propellers slashed his shoulder, chest, and windpipe.

Emilio immediately shut down the engines and leaped into the water. Clark was floating facedown on the surface. "I was worried about barracudas and sharks. There was blood all over the place, and I'm thinking my legs are going to be eaten in front of my wife," Emilio recalled. "But it's someone's life and you have to try to help."[2]

Gloria called 9-1-1 on her cell phone. Other boaters helped get Clark and Green to shore, where they were rushed to a waiting ambulance. Maynard Clark died before reaching the hospital.

Emilio, who does not drink, knew that alcohol was often a factor in boating accidents. He wanted it on record that he had not been drinking. He went to the Coast Guard station and asked for a blood test. He had no problem passing the test. Only bottled water was found in his boat.

Word of the accident spread quickly, especially because a celebrity was involved. Reporters from all over the world began calling Miami for details. Gloria was upset enough by Maynard Clark's death. The media attention only made it worse.

"Why is everybody asking about us?" Gloria said to Captain Mike Lamphear of the Florida Marine Patrol. "This is a bright young man with a future lost, what about him?"[3]

Gloria called Clark's family in Rhode Island to express her grief. "It's the hardest thing I've ever had to do in my life," she said. "But the truck driver who hit me never called me. And I could never forget that."[4]

> *Word of the accident spread quickly, especially because a celebrity was involved.*

Gloria had always been frustrated with Florida's weak boating laws. The state did not require any licensing or training for someone renting a personal watercraft. Anyone over the age of fourteen could drive one. "It's like giving someone a motorcycle and not telling them how to drive it," said Emilio. "And with a wet bike, you have no brakes."[5] The Estefans did not allow fifteen-year-old Nayib to drive one without a responsible adult nearby to supervise.

Florida state legislators had already defeated fourteen bills designed to strengthen boating laws. They were afraid the added restrictions would hurt the state's tourist industry. But they had never dealt with Gloria Estefan before. Maynard Clark's death spurred her into action. Fighting for stronger boating laws was a way to make something positive come from Clark's death.

In February 1996, Estefan spoke to the Florida House Committee on Natural Resources. Anyone who thought she was just a celebrity looking for publicity soon saw how serious she was. She told the committee that she had been a boater for ten years. She had taken courses in navigation, seamanship, and piloting to improve her skills.[6] She emphasized how important it was for boaters and people on personal watercraft to be educated on how to operate them.

Anyone who thought she was just a celebrity looking for publicity soon saw how serious she was.

Estefan's impassioned speech helped sway the Florida legislature. They passed a bill requiring boaters under the age of sixteen to take a safety course before they could drive a boat. It also required twenty minutes of training for anyone renting even a small personal watercraft. Lives may have been saved because Estefan cared enough to speak out on an issue she believed in.

Gloria, Emilio, Nayib, and Emily in 2001.

After her success with the Florida legislature, Estefan could turn her attention to other projects. Construction was under way on a second house next to their mansion on Star Island. The beautiful $6 million addition would have a flowing waterfall in front, a movie theater inside, a guest cottage in back, and an indoor home for the pets. "I love to stay home, so I figure I'll make a resort at my house," Estefan said.[7]

One of the less enthusiastic construction workers for a time was fifteen-year-old Nayib. He had to work from 6 A.M. to 3 P.M. five days a week as punishment for a prank that got him expelled from school. While attending the elite Gulliver Prep School, Nayib had called the home of a schoolmate and pretended to be the school principal. He told the boy's mother that her son had

Discipline and Pranksters

Emily and Nayib Estefan have very different personalities. Emily is shy in front of strangers, just as Gloria was as a child. Nayib has his father's outgoing personality. Emilio and Nayib are both pranksters and love being the center of attention. Gloria and Emilio do not believe in spanking their children. This means Gloria sometimes had to resort to creative discipline to keep her playful son in line. "Nayib hates writing lines over and over. One punishment he didn't like was repeatedly writing, 'I will not moon the tour boats that pass by.' After that he never did it again," Gloria said.[8]

been expelled for participating in a food fight. The call was traced to Nayib's phone.

In 1996 Estefan released the album *Destiny*. The songs were sung in English but were backed with Latin rhythms. Gloria wrote most of the songs for *Destiny*. The love she felt for her daughter inspired her to write "Along Came You." Two-year-old Emily was in the studio the day the song was recorded. "When we got to the lullaby, she started cooing and singing along. It was the most beautiful thing I ever heard. It just had to be on the record," Estefan said.[9]

Destiny also included "Reach," the official song of the 1996 Summer Olympic Games held in Atlanta, Georgia. Gloria and songwriter Diane Warren had written "Reach" in only twenty minutes. "The song just came to us," Gloria said. "Diane said 'What do you think of "Reach" as a title?' I thought about it for a minute and realized it was incredible."[10]

The word "reach" had a personal meaning for Estefan. It reminded her of her struggle to recover from the accident that nearly paralyzed her. "Writing the song took me back to my first night back on stage after a year of recovery, which was almost like winning a gold medal—it was the most euphoric feeling of victory I have ever felt in my entire life."[11]

The members of the Olympic Committee were surprised when they heard "Reach" for the first time. They had not told the women that the slogan for the 1996 Olympics was "Higher, Stronger, Faster." Yet in

Estefan sang from atop a high platform at the close of the 1996 Summer Olympic Games.

the chorus of "Reach" were the words, "If I could reach higher, I'm gonna be stronger. . . ."[12]

A dark cloud hung over the Olympics that year. Someone hid a bomb in a backpack and left it in Atlanta's Centennial Park. The explosion killed one person and injured many more. Estefan did not let the fear of another attack keep her from performing at the closing ceremony. "The world is ruled by either fear or love, and we cannot allow ourselves to be intimidated by fear," she said.[13]

Estefan's inspiring performance of "Reach" was seen by an estimated 3 billion television viewers around the world. But it was her performance of "Conga" that sent the athletes into a frenzy. Athletes from all over the world joined together in a long conga line. "I thought, wow, what a great choreography. I thought it was planned. But then the tower I was singing from started shaking and I thought, 'Great, first the bus, then the boat, now the tower,'" Estefan said.[14]

Estefan had not been on tour since *Into the Light* five years earlier. Now she needed to promote her new album, *Destiny*. She began her *Evolution Tour*, which would take her to forty-two cities in the United States and ten countries.

Evolution had a dramatic opening. As Afro-Cuban dancers performed on stage, a large steel ball covered in white passed over the audience. The crowd went wild as the cover was dropped, revealing Estefan inside the metal cage. This spectacle did not always go smoothly. At a concert in Holland, the ball refused to move. With her typical sense of humor, Estefan began singing "I think I'm stuck in the ball now!" She added, "They had to pull me out, but it was funny. You've got to laugh at those things."[15]

Evolution was a family affair. As Gloria sang "Along Came You," family pictures dating back to her parents' marriage were shown on giant screens. When the song finished, Nayib led tiny Emily onto the stage to join Gloria. Nayib appeared onstage again to play the drums for his mother's closing number. Nothing is more important to Gloria than her family, and she enjoyed introducing them to the world.

Gloria received another special honor in 1996 when she was inducted into the National Academy of Popular Music's Songwriters Hall of Fame. She was given the academy's Hitmaker Award. "That's a big thing for me," Estefan explained. "Because most people don't even know we write our own things."[16]

Also in 1996, *Billboard* magazine awarded its first Spirit of Hope award to honor recording stars for their work with civic, community, and humanitarian organizations. Gloria Estefan was the first person to win the Spirit of Hope award. She was recognized for her caring attitude toward people in difficult situations.

Gloria's success with her music mirrored the success the Estefans were having in their business enterprises. In November 1997, they opened Bongo's Cuban Café in Walt Disney World in Orlando, Florida. The two-story pineapple-shaped restaurant was designed to look like a Cuban mansion from the 1950s. Tourists flock to the 500-seat restaurant to enjoy the Cuban dishes that Gloria loves.

> **Nothing is more important to Gloria than her family.**

In 1998 Estefan released her next album, *gloria!* Estefan used the album to bring back the feelings of the seventies. She wanted her last album of the twentieth century to be a celebration that would make everyone feel good. The lively mix of Cuban and Latin disco

The album *gloria!* was launched with a big party at Studio 54, a popular disco in New York City.

party music did just that. It gave Estefan's listeners a chance to let loose and have fun.

Estefan was offered another opportunity to sing for Pope John Paul II when he visited Cuba in January 1998. She turned down the invitation. "My going there would have turned a beautiful spiritual thing into a political thing. . . . I would have asked for permission from the Cuban government, which I'm not about to do, and it just would have been a slap into the face of my father and everything he fought for."[17]

Estefan had achieved success as a singer, a performer, and a businesswoman. Now she was ready for a new challenge. She began taking acting lessons. "I'm not gonna quit singing, because that's who I am. But it's nice to grow and to keep moving into different things," Estefan said.[18]

Estefan turned down the lead role in the movie *Evita*. She did not want the responsibility of starring in her first movie. She also did not want to be away from her family on location in Hungary for a long period of time. The role went to Madonna.

Instead, Estefan took a small part as the friend of Meryl Streep's character in the 1999 movie *Music of the Heart*. The movie portrayed a real-life teacher fighting to bring music education to inner-city schools in New York City. It was a subject close to Estefan's heart. "I think teaching children music is so important, just as important as math or social studies in terms of their development."[19] Estefan sang with the band *NSYNC to record the title song for the movie. Their song, "Music of the Heart," was nominated for an Academy Award as best original song. They did not win the Oscar, but Gloria and *NSYNC got to perform the song for the television broadcast of the awards show.

Estefan's many talents take her into many different areas. The one area she usually keeps to herself is politics. But late in 1999, a controversy over a small boy threw her into the political spotlight once again.

10

Giving Back

In November 1999, a young Cuban mother fled her homeland, taking her five-year-old son, Elian, on a boat journey in search of freedom in the United States. During a frightening night, the boat capsized, spilling its twelve passengers into the dark water between Cuba and Florida. Elian's mother drowned, but not before she strapped her son into an inner tube. On Thanksgiving morning, two fishermen found Elian floating alone, still inside the inner tube.

Relatives in Miami took Elian into their home. But Elian's father and grandparents loved him and wanted him returned home to Cuba. The small boy with the big brown eyes sparked a controversy that raged across two countries. Most Cuban exiles in Miami thought Elian should stay in the United States to fulfill his mother's dream of freedom. Others felt that nothing was as important as reuniting Elian with his father. Elian stayed in Miami for many months while a judge decided his future.

As someone who had been forced to leave Cuba herself, Gloria Estefan joined the controversy. She told Rosie O'Donnell during a magazine interview, "I couldn't shy away from it, because I'm a Cuban and I'm living in the city. How could I not have an opinion?"[1] Estefan thought that Elian's father should have come immediately to be with his son in the United States. She wanted psychologists to evaluate Elian to determine what was best for him.[2]

After four months of controversy, a federal judge finally made the decision. He ordered Elian to be returned to his father in Cuba. Juan Miguel Gonzales came to the United States to get his son. But the Miami relatives were not ready to give him up.

April 13, 2000, was set as the deadline for Elian to be returned to his father. That day, hundreds of protesters gathered around the home of Elian's relatives. As their chants became more heated, Estefan was asked to speak to the group to calm them down. "I know we Cubans are very passionate but we don't want people to confuse loud passion for violence," she said.[3] She urged that Elian's story be heard in a court of law.

When no agreement could be reached, U.S. Attorney General Janet Reno took drastic action. She sent armed agents from the Immigration and Naturalization Services to take Elian back. On April 22, agents burst into the relatives' home in the middle of the night. They found a terrified Elian hiding in a closet. In spite of the frightening experience, Elian seemed happy to be with his father again. They eventually returned to Cuba.

Estefan was upset with the way the incident had been handled. "Today is a very sad day for the United States and the world; when once again we show our children that conflicts are resolved using guns, violence and terror instead of communication and peaceful negotiation."[4]

During the Elian Gonzales controversy, something else was getting a lot of attention—the beginning of a new century. As the year 1999 came to an end, the world was looking ahead to the millennium. In Miami, thousands gathered for Gloria Estefan's Millennium Concert

Escape from Cuba

For years, thousands of Cubans have risked their lives to get to the United States. Some set out in makeshift boats or rafts pieced together from scraps. Others pay smugglers with speedboats to race them across the ninety miles of water. All have the same goal. By law, if they can set foot on land in America, they can ask for permission to stay. Most of the escapees are unsuccessful. If they are caught by the Cuban Coast Guard or the United States Coast Guard, they are returned to Cuba. All too many die in their attempt to escape when their boats break apart in rough seas, leaving them to drown. But to the escapees, the chance to live a better life in a free country is considered worth the risk.

Spectacular. Besides ushering in the year 2000, her concert celebrated the opening of the new American Airlines Arena. Estefan sang and danced beneath a glittering revolving disco ball. Her performance of English and Spanish songs was broadcast on television worldwide. Gloria's entire family joined her onstage as balloons and confetti dropped at the stroke of midnight. The lively celebration was a fitting beginning to the twenty-first century and Miami's newest attraction.

The new century also brought a new album for Estefan. Her first two Spanish-language albums, *Mi Tierra* and *Abriendo Puertas*, had both received Grammys. In 2000 she added a third Spanish album—*Alma Caribena* (Caribbean Soul). It featured songs that blend the musical sounds of Cuba, Puerto Rico, the Dominican Republic, and Panama. "Latin music culture is so rich and so diverse, there's no way to capture it all on one record," Estefan explained.[5]

Estefan used a different approach when working on the songs for this album. "I almost imagined myself back in my grandma's kitchen, playing guitar for her and just emoting," Estefan said. "There is heavy drama in this album. I definitely think it comes from growing up in a Cuban household."[6] Her approach worked. *Alma Caribena* won a Grammy for Best Tropical Latin Album.

Estefan had planned to go on tour in 2000 to promote *Alma Caribena*. But by that time, Emily was getting ready to start school. Estefan wanted her daughter's life to be as normal as possible. She also wanted to stay home for a while to spend time with her children. Estefan took a break from the hectic pace of her career and devoted herself to the job of being a mom.

Over the years, Estefan's feelings toward motherhood had changed. When Nayib was born, Estefan was pouring her energies into building her career. But there were too many missed Little League games, and a painful separation when she had to go on tour without him. By the time Emily was born, Estefan had reached a different point in her life. She had achieved a level of fame far beyond anything she could have dreamed of. With her career firmly established, Estefan decided to take the time to step back and relish every moment of raising her daughter.

"I'm a mother before anything in my life," Estefan emphasized. "I took care of my dad before I was an actual mom. I took care of my sister. I'm maternal; it's a very strong instinct in me."[7]

Estefan may have been taking a career break, but she was not idle. In addition to promoting *Alma Caribeña*, she took on another movie role. Estefan joined her friend Andy Garcia for the HBO movie *For Love or Country: The Arturo Sandoval Story*. The movie was based on the life of jazz trumpeter Arturo Sandoval, who fled Cuba with his family. Estefan played a friend of Sandoval's wife. As with her first movie, the subject matter for this film was close to Estefan's heart. "It's very political and about Cuba. I felt it important to participate

Estefan filmed a television special, *Caribbean Soul*, to promote the release of *Alma Caribena*, an album celebrating the diversity of Latin music.

because it's the first time, I think people will get the true picture of what goes on there."[8]

In June 2001, Gloria and Emilio returned to the National Academy of Popular Music's Songwriters Hall of Fame. This time the academy presented them with the prestigious Sammy Cahn Lifetime Achievement Award. They were the first Hispanics to receive this honor.[9]

On September 11, 2001, the entire world watched in horror as terrorists flew passenger planes into the Twin Towers at the World Trade Center in New York City. Another plane hit the Pentagon in Washington, D.C. A fourth plane crashed in a field in Pennsylvania before it reached its Washington, D.C., destination. Thousands of innocent people lost their lives in these attacks. Once again, tragedy spurred the Estefans into action. Emilio and Gian Marco wrote the song *"El Ultimo Adios"* (The Last Goodbye). Gloria was among nearly sixty Latin musicians who sang the song at a tribute held on September 28, 2001. The song was released in both English and Spanish. All the

> *"I'm a mother before anything in my life."*
>
> —Gloria Estefan

proceeds went to the Red Cross and the United Way to help the victims and their families.

Estefan's three-year break allowed her to spend more time writing songs. The result was the album *Unwrapped*, released in September 2003. It was Estefan's first album in English in six years. It was also her most personal. Estefan wrote the lyrics to all fourteen songs on the album. She also helped produce it. "There's a lot of my life in there," Estefan said. "We wanted to create almost a musical picture book of my past life."[10]

Even the cover for *Unwrapped* was personal. It showed Estefan wearing little more than body paint and blue glitter. Lyrics from the album were written backward across her body, showing how they would look written from the inside out. On the back cover, the long scar she had kept hidden since her accident was clearly visible. "It's there, scars and all," she said. "That's what this album is."[11]

> **Once again, tragedy spurred the Estefans into action.**

Estefan introduced *Unwrapped* while filling in for Celine Dion at Caesar's Palace in Las Vegas. Estefan's only concern about performing in the famous theater was the slanted stage. "The biggest fear is that I will trip and roll down the stage. They'll have to put a net down there to catch me," she joked.[12]

Unwrapped also gave Estefan a focus for the final tour of her career. It had been eight years since she had taken her *Evolution Tour* on the road. She admitted that when she stopped touring she would miss the interaction with her fans, but not the exhausting nature of touring. "It's physically grueling, like training for an

As she announced that her 2004–2005 concert tour would be her last, the "Queen of Latin Pop" looked forward to a future rich with new challenges.

Olympic event," she said."[13] Her days on tour consisted of working, sleeping, doing the show, and little else.

Giving up touring did not mean Estefan was giving up her musical career. She will still perform at one-time shows, charity events, and prolonged engagements at a single location, as she did in Las Vegas.

The versatile performer looked forward to pursuing a number of other interests. "I would love to be able to produce some music. I love being behind the camera. I've got some ideas for a show I'd love to do . . . and I'd love to have more time to write more for other artists," Estefan said.[14]

Estefan has other types of writing planned, too, including a children's book and an autobiography. The children's book (published in 2005 in both English and Spanish editions) features the adventures of her real-life pet bulldog Noelle. A song about Noelle, written and recorded by Estefan, accompanies each book.

Another of Gloria Estefan's projects is to write the screenplay for *Who's Sorry Now?*, the autobiography of 1950s pop singer Connie Francis. Like Gloria, Francis had much tragedy to overcome in her life. She asked Gloria to make a movie of her life story. When the screenplay is finished, Gloria plans to play the part of Connie Francis.

Gloria and Emilio have accumulated great wealth as a result of their talent, hard work, and determination to succeed. But it is their desire to use their money to help others that earned them the love and respect of the world.

Most of the Estefans' charity work is handled through the Gloria Estefan Foundation. Gloria would rather call it an "anti-foundation" because of its low-key approach to raising money. "I hate bothering people for money. So, I took three songs of mine—"Always Tomorrow," "Coming Out of the Dark" and "Path of the Right Love"—and all the royalties I receive go to the foundation."[15] In addition to all the donations from the Estefans, Gloria's fans donate money to the foundation each year on her birthday.

The Gloria Estefan Foundation contributes about $500,000 a year to various causes and charities. It has helped hurricane victims in the Caribbean and many children's charities around the world. It has paid for band instruments for poor schools and purchased badly needed hospital equipment. Estefan's experiences with a broken back have made her a strong supporter of the Miami Project to Cure Paralysis. She and Emilio have helped raise more than $40 million for the center, which specializes in spinal-cord injury research.[16]

> *Giving up touring did not mean Gloria was giving up her musical career.*

Gloria Estefan has it all. She is beautiful, talented, intelligent, and wealthy. She has a solid marriage, two wonderful children, and the love of millions of fans.

The five-time Grammy Award-winning singer has sold more than 70 million albums and CDs worldwide and has won too many awards to list. As the "Queen of Latin Pop," Gloria has brought Latin music into the mainstream. On the side, she has dabbled in movies, become a successful businesswoman, and helped millions of people through her charity work.

Quincy Jones, the famous musician, film producer, and songwriter, once commented, "My teacher Nadia Boulanger once told me that 'an artist can never be more than he or she is as a human being.' That sums up Gloria Estefan to a tee. The only thing that surpasses her artistry is the size of her heart and her compassion for others."[17]

Some would call Estefan lucky, but looking at her life makes it obvious that her extraordinary success does not come from luck. It comes from her willingness to tackle challenges head-on. It comes from the love and appreciation she has for the millions of fans that have put her where she is today. It comes from her desire to turn tragedies into opportunities to make the world a better place to live. And it comes from her steadfast belief in staying true to her roots and her values. The combination has brought Gloria Estefan incredible success as a performer and businesswoman, but mostly, as a person.

Chronology

1957—Gloria Marie Fajardo is born in Havana, Cuba, on September 1.

1959—The Fajardo family flees Cuba for Miami, Florida, after Fidel Castro overthrows the Cuban dictator Fulgencio Batista.

1961—José Fajardo is captured during the Bay of Pigs invasion and becomes a political prisoner in Cuba.

1962—José Fajardo is released from prison in Cuba and returns to Miami.

1963—José Fajardo joins the U.S. Army and moves his family to San Antonio, Texas; Gloria's sister, Rebecca, is born.

1966—José Fajardo fights in Vietnam War; his family moves back to Miami.

1968—José Fajardo returns from Vietnam and is diagnosed with multiple sclerosis; Gloria begins caring for her father and younger sister after school each day.

1975—Gloria attends the University of Miami; joins Emilio Estefan's band, the Miami Latin Boys; band changes its name to Miami Sound Machine.

1978—Gloria graduates from the University of Miami; marries Emilio Estefan on September 2.

1980—José Fajardo dies; Gloria's son, Nayib, is born; Miami Sound Machine signs a recording contract with Discos CBS International.

1984—Miami Sound Machine records "Dr. Beat," written by drummer Kiki Garcia; the band records its first all-English album, *Eyes of Innocence*.

1985—Kiki Garcia writes "Conga," which makes crossover history by appearing on four pop charts at the same time.

1987—*Let It Loose* is released with the band's new name, Gloria Estefan and the Miami Sound Machine; Emilio Estefan stops performing with the band.

1988—"Anything for You" becomes Gloria Estefan's first number-one pop hit.

1989—*Cuts Both Ways* is released with only Gloria Estefan's name on the album cover; she wins American Billboard Award for Songwriter of the Year.

1990—Estefan breaks her back in a bus accident in March and spends the rest of the year in rehabilitation.

1991—*Into the Light* is released; Estefan begins her comeback tour; "Coming Out of the Dark" reaches number one on the pop charts.

1992—Hurricane Andrew strikes Florida, and Estefan works in the relief effort; she is appointed as a delegate to the United Nations by President George H. W. Bush.

1994—Estefan wins her first Grammy when *Mi Tierra* is named Best Tropical Album; daughter Emily Marie Estefan is born.

1995—The driver of a personal watercraft is killed when he collides with the Estefans' boat.

1996—"Reach" becomes the official song of the 1996 Summer Olympic Games; Estefan sings at the closing ceremonies; she receives Hitmaker Award from the National Academy of Popular Music's Songwriters Hall of Fame.

1999—Estefan makes her movie debut in *Music of the Heart*.

2001—Gloria and Emilio Estefan become the first Hispanics to receive the Sammy Cahn Lifetime Achievement Award by the National Academy of Popular Music's Songwriters Hall of Fame.

2004—Estefan begins *Rewrapped* tour, the final tour of her career.

2005—Estefan publishes a children's book about her pet bulldog Noelle.

Discography

Albums and Selected Songs

Live Again/Renacer, 1978

Miami Sound Machine: Imported, 1979

Miami Sound Machine, 1980

Otra Vez, 1981

Rio, 1982

A Toda Máquina, 1984

Eyes of Innocence, 1984

Primitive Love, 1985
"Words Get in the Way"
"Bad Boy"
"Conga"

Let It Loose, 1987
"Anything for You"
"1-2-3"
"Rhythm Is Gonna Get You"
"Can't Stay Away from You"

Cuts Both Ways, 1989
"Don't Wanna Lose You"
"Here We Are"
"Get on Your Feet"

Into the Light, 1991
"Coming Out of the Dark"
"Live for Loving You"

Greatest Hits, 1992

Mi Tierra, 1993

Christmas Through Your Eyes, 1993

Hold Me, Thrill Me, Kiss Me, 1994
"Everlasting Love"
"Turn the Beat Around"

Abriendo Puertas, 1995

Destiny, 1996
"Reach"
"You'll Be Mine" (Party Time)

gloria!, 1998

Alma Caribena, 2000

Unwrapped, 2003

Amor Y Suerte, 2004

Videography

Homecoming Concert (1989)

Don't Stop (1989)

Evolution (1990)

Coming Out of the Dark (1990)

Into the Light World Tour (1991)

Everlasting Gloria (1995)

Evolution Tour '96: Live in Miami (1996)

Don't Stop (1998)

Live in Atlantis (2000)

Que Siga la Tradicion (2000)

For Love of Country: The Arturo Sandoval Story (2000)

Live & Unwrapped (2004)

Chapter Notes

CHAPTER 1. A HAUNTING FEAR

1. Kathryn Casey, "My Miracle," *Ladies Home Journal*, August 1990, p. 152.
2. Ibid.
3. Melina Gerosa, "My Song of Love," *Ladies Home Journal*, April 1997, p. 176.
4. Steve Dougherty, "One Step at a Time," *People Weekly*, June 25, 1990, p. 78.
5. Ibid.
6. Anthony DeStefano, *Gloria Estefan . . . From Tragedy to Triumph* (New York: Signet, 1997), p. 57.
7. Casey, p. 152.
8. Ibid.
9. Dougherty, "One Step at a Time," p. 80.
10. Casey, p. 152.
11. Steve Dougherty, "Singer Gloria Estefan Takes Her First Steps to Recovery After a Frightening Bus Crash," *People Weekly*, April 9, 1990, p. 2.
12. Casey, p. 152.
13. Dougherty, "Singer Gloria Estefan," p. 82.
14. *Gloria Estefan: Into the Light World Tour*, Emilio Estefan, Jr., Executive Producer, Sony Music Video Enterprises, 1991 (videocassette).
15. Casey, p. 155.
16. Dougherty, "Singer Gloria Estefan," p. 82.
17. DeStefano, p. 68.

Chapter 2. "No Children, No Pets, No Cubans"

1. John Cummins, *The Voyage of Christopher Columbus* (New York: St. Martin's Press, 1992), p.108.
2. Anthony DeStefano, *Gloria Estefan . . . From Tragedy to Triumph* (New York: Signet, 1997), p. 12.
3. *Dateline NBC*, "Estefan Returns with New CD," September 21, 2003, <http://msnbc.msn.com/id/3079850> (February 26, 2004), p. 2.
4. Mark Fest, "Interview with Gloria Estefan," September 8, 1988, *US News for German Media*, <http://www.fest.net/marc/estefan/> (February 29, 2004), p. 3.
5. Peter Castro, "Little Glorita, Happy at Last," *People Weekly*, August 12, 1996, p. 60.
6. *Dateline NBC*, p. 3.
7. Leonard Pitts, Jr., "Miami's Patron Saint," *Entertainment Weekly*, July 30, 1993, p. 55.
8. Castro, p. 60.
9. Hans van Willigenburg, "Interview with Gloria Estefan," May 11, 2000, "Koffietijd" ("Coffee Break") on RTL4 (German television station), <http://www.geocities.com/sunsetstrip/stadium/8154/koffietijdtranscript.html> (June 21, 2003).
10. Rosie O'Donnell, "Interview with Gloria Estefan," *Rosie*, April 2002, p. 71.
11. Michelle Genz, "Golden Girl," *Miami Herald*, May 31, 1998, Tropic Section, <http://www.fiu.edu/~fcf/gloria53198.html> (February 25, 2004).
12. Daniel Rubin, "My happiest memory . . . ," *Parents*, March 1998, p. 134.
13. DeStefano, p. 20.
14. van Willigenburg.
15. DeStefano, p. 20.

16. Genz.

17. "Gloria Estefan," Divastation.com, <http://www.divastation.com/gloria_estefan/estefan_bio.html> (September 9, 2004).

18. "Gloria Estefan," *Newsmakers 1991*, Gale Research, 1991, <http://galenet.galegroup.com/servlet/SRC?txba=Gloria+Estefan&vrsn=3.0&slb=SU&locID=txshrpub100321&srchtp=basic&c=2&ste=21&tbst=ts_bsc&tab=1&docNum=K1618000863&fail=0&bConts=15> (February 25, 2004).

19. Melina Gerosa, "My Song of Love," *Ladies Home Journal*, April 1997, p. 120.

20. "Gloria Estefan," Divastation.com.

CHAPTER 3.   PRINCE CHARMING

1. Sheryl Berk, "Livin' la vida Gloria," *McCall's*, November 1999, p. 53.

2. Hans van Willigenburg, "Interview with Gloria Estefan," May 11, 2000, "Koffietijd" ("Coffee Break") on RTL4 (German television station), <http://www.geocities.com/sunsetstrip/stadium/8154/koffietijdtranscript.html> (June 21, 2003).

3. Judith Graham, ed., *1995: Current Biography Yearbook* (New York: The H. W. Wilson Co., 1995), p. 149.

4. Anthony DeStefano, *Gloria Estefan . . . From Tragedy to Triumph* (New York: Signet, 1997), p. 28.

5. Cynthia Corzo, "Dynamic Duo," *Hispanic*, May 1999, p. 20.

6. DeStefano, p. 29.

7. Michelle Genz, "Golden Girl," *Miami Herald*, May 31, 1998, <http://www.fiu.edu/~fcf/gloria53198.html> (February 25, 2004).

8. Grace Catalano, *Gloria Estefan* (New York: St. Martin's Press, 1991), p. 45.

9. DeStefano, p. 32.

10. Catalano, p. 44.

11. Jesse Nash and George Flowers, "Playing Dual Roles in a Sound Relationship," *Billboard*, April 21, 1990, p. M-7.

12. DeStefano, p. 33.

13. "The Touch of Platinum," *South Florida*, 1996, <http://www.beepworld.de/members27/gloria-latindiva-magazine/1996southfloria.htm> (June 21, 2003).

14. Daisann McLane, "The Power and the Gloria," *Rolling Stone*, June 14, 1990, p. 74.

15. Ibid.

16. Catalano, p. 49.

17. Judith Graham, ed., *1995: Current Biography Yearbook* (New York: The H. W. Wilson Co., 1995), p. 149.

18. Catalano, p. 52.

CHAPTER 4. THE MACHINE STARTS ROLLING

1. Anthony DeStefano, *Gloria Estefan . . . From Tragedy to Triumph* (New York: Signet, 1997), p. 33.

2. Mark Fest, "Interview with Gloria Estefan," September 8, 1988, *US News for German Media*, <http://www.fest.net/marc/estefan/> (February 29, 2004).

3. Ibid.

4. Jesse Nash and George Flowers, "Playing Dual Roles in a Sound Relationship," *Billboard*, April 21, 1990, p. M-7.

5. Diane Loomins, "Gloria Estefan—An Intimate Conversation With a Pop Music Visionary," *Body Mind Spirit*, 1996, <http://www.beepworld.de/members27/gloria-latindiva-magazine/1996bms.htm> (February 25, 2004).

6. Dan Le Batard, "A Blaze of Gloria," *New Woman*, December 1997, <http://www.geocities.com/jetpack7/migloria/geart/blazeofglo97.rtf> (February 25, 2004).

7. Grace Catalano, *Gloria Estefan* (New York: St. Martin's Press, 1991), p. 53.

8. Judith Graham, ed., *1995: Current Biography Yearbook* (New York: The H. W. Wilson Co., 1995), p. 150.

9. DeStefano, p. 38.

10. Ibid.

11. Linda Marx, "Throw the Switch on the Miami Sound Machine, and Pop Go the Hit Singles," *People Weekly*, October 27, 1986, p. 77.

CHAPTER 5. CROSSOVER!

1. Anthony DeStefano, *Gloria Estefan . . . From Tragedy to Triumph* (New York: Signet, 1997), p. 40.

2. Judith Graham, ed., *1995: Current Biography Yearbook*, (New York: The H. W. Wilson Co, 1995), p. 151.

3. ABC News Specials, "The Latin Beat," Interview with John Quinones, September 7, 1999, <http://abcnews.go.com/onair/2020/transcripts/sp990907_latinbeat_trans2.html> (May 13, 2003).

4. Jesse Nash and George Flowers, "The Sound Machine Time Machine," *Billboard*, April 21, 1990, p. M-10.

5. Lee Ann Obringer, "How Top 40 Radio Works," <http://ibs.howstuffworks.com/ibs/orlwx/top-401.htm> (February 25, 2004).

6. Robert La Franco, "Salsa, Inc.," *Forbes*, September 22, 1997, p. 154.

7. Graham, p. 151.

8. Grace Catalano, *Gloria Estefan* (New York: St. Martin's Press, 1991), p. 80.

9. Judy Cantor, "Shine On, Crescent Moon," *Miami New Times*, September 7, 1994, <http://www.miaminewtimes.com/issues/1994-09-07/feature.html/print.html> (September 25, 2004).

10. Catalano, p. 82.

11. Ibid.

12. Graham, p. 150.

13. Linda Marx, "Throw the Switch on the Miami Sound Machine, and Pop Go the Hit Singles," *People Weekly*, October 27, 1986, p. 77.

CHAPTER 6. LETTING IT LOOSE

1. Jesse Nash and George Flowers, "CBS/Epic: Marketing the Platinum Moon Over Miami Sound Machine," *Billboard*, April 21, 1990, p. M-16.

2. "Gloria Estefan," 1998, <http://www.beepworld.de/members27/gloria-latindiva-magazine/1998hx.htm> (February 25, 2004).

3. Jesse Nash and George Flowers, "Playing Dual Roles in a Sound Relationship," *Billboard*, April 21, 1990, p. M-17.

4. Anthony DeStefano, *Gloria Estefan . . . From Tragedy to Triumph* (New York: Signet, 1997), p. 47.

5. Ibid.

6. Grace Catalano, *Gloria Estefan* (New York: St. Martin's Press, 1991), p. 148.

7. DeStefano, p. 44.

8. Judy Cantor, "Shine On, Crescent Moon," *Miami New Times*, September 7, 1994, <http://www.miaminewtimes.com/issues/1994-09-07/feature.html/print.html> (February 25, 2004).

9. Laura Morice, "Gloria Hallelujah!" *McCall's*, July 1995, p. 73.

10. Catalano, p. 79.

11. Ibid., p. 127.

12. Kathryn Casey, "My Miracle," *Ladies Home Journal*, August 1990, p. 100.

CHAPTER 7.   COMING OUT OF THE DARK

1. Juan Carlos Cato, "Fans Crowd Around as Estefan Returns Home for Recovery," *Miami Herald*, April 5, 1990, p. 1B.
2. Laura Morice, "Gloria Hallelujah!" *McCall's*, July 1995, p. 72.
3. Steve Dougherty, "One Step at a Time," *People Weekly*, June 25, 1990, p. 78.
4. Patti Davis, "Life in Tune: Gloria Estefan Discovers the Power of Faith and Love," *Living Fit*, April 1998, <http://www.geocities.com/jetpack7/migloria/ geart/lifeintune98.rtf> (February 25, 2003).
5. Dougherty, "One Step at a Time," p. 78.
6. Steve Dougherty, "A Year After Her Brush With Disaster, Gloria Estefan Dances Out of the Dark With a New Album and World Tour," *People Weekly*, February 18, 1991, p. 118.
7. Ibid., p. 2.

CHAPTER 8.   AN AMERICAN HEAD AND A CUBAN HEART

1. John Lannert, "Emilio Branches Out," *Billboard*, September 26, 1998, p. 70.
2. Ibid.
3. Leonard Pitts, Jr., "Hurricane Relief," *Miami Herald*, September 25, 1992, p. 22G.
4. Ibid.
5. Cynthia Corzo, "Dynamic Duo," *Hispanic*, May 1999, p. 18.
6. Pam Lambert, "Miami spells hurricane relief G-L-O-R-I-A," *People Weekly*, October 12, 1992, p. 47.
7. Corzo, p. 20.

8. <http://www.state.gov/secretary/rm/2002/14236.htm> (February 24, 2004).

9. Pitts, p. 22-G.

10. Corzo, p. 20.

11. Anthony DeStefano, *Gloria Estefan . . . From Tragedy to Triumph* (New York: Signet, 1997), p. 109.

12. Ibid., p. 110.

13. Melina Gerosa, "My Song of Love," *Ladies Home Journal*, April 1997, p. 178.

14. Christopher John Farley, "From a Cuban Heart," *Time*, July 8, 1996, p. 68.

15. Lannert, p. 70.

16. Laura Morice, "Gloria Hallelujah!" *McCall's*, July 1995, p. 70.

17. Kathleen Sampey, "Star Watch: For Gloria Estefan, 'Everything's Funny'," *South Coast Today*, NewStandard, July 5, 1996, <http://www.s-t.com/daily/07-05-96/b011i035.htm> (May 13, 2003).

18. DeStefano, p. 123.

CHAPTER 9. REACHING HIGHER

1. Peter Castro and Cindy Dampier, "Water Hazard: A Fatal Crash Involving Gloria Estefan Reveals the Peril of Wet Bikes," *People Weekly*, October 9, 1995, p. 65.

2. Peter Castro, "Little Glorita, Happy at Last," *People Weekly*, August 12, 1996, p. 60.

3. Anthony DeStefano, *Gloria Estefan . . . From Tragedy to Triumph* (New York: Signet, 1997), p. 127.

4. Michelle Genz, "Golden Girl," *Miami Herald*, May 31, 1998, <http://www.fiu.edu/~fcf/gloria53198.html> (February 25, 2004).

5. Castro and Dampier, p. 3.

6. DeStefano, p. 132.

7. Laura Morice, "Gloria Hallelujah!" *McCall's*, July 1995, p. 73.

8. DeStefano, p. 148.

9. Catherine McEvily Harris, "Gloria's *Destiny*," *Shape*, October 1996, p. 131.

10. Diane Loomins, "Gloria Estefan—An Intimate Conversation With a Pop Music Visionary," *Body Mind Spirit*, 1996, <http://www.beepworld.de/members27/gloria-latindiva-magazine/1996bms.htm> (February 25, 2004).

11. Harris, p. 131.

12. Castro, "Little Glorita, Happy at Last," p. 60.

13. Lydia Martin, "The Evolution of Pop Diva Gloria Estefan Transcends Power and Fame," *Knight Ridder/Tribune News Service*, September 19, 1996, p. 3.

14. Melina Gerosa, "My Song of Love," *Ladies Home Journal*, April 1997, p. 120.

15. Kathleen Sampey, "Star Watch: For Gloria Estefan, 'Everything's Funny'," *South Coast Today*, NewStandard, July 5, 1996, <http://www.s-t.com/daily/07-05-96/b011i035.htm> (May 13, 2003).

16. Mark Fest, "Interview with Gloria Estefan," September 8, 1988, *US News for German Media*, <http://www.fest.net/marc/estefan/> (February 29, 2004).

17. Ibid.

18. Sheryl Berk, "Livin' la vida Gloria," *McCall's*, November 1999, p. 52.

19. Peter Castro, "Clothes Encounter," *People Weekly*, November 6, 1995.

CHAPTER 10. GIVING BACK

1. Rosie O'Donnell, "Interview with Gloria Estefan," *Rosie*, April, 2002, p. 72.

2. "Larry King Interviews Gloria Estefan and Jesse Jackson, Jr. on the Elian Gonzales Custody Case," *Larry King Live*,

CNN, March 30, 2000, <http://www.geocities.com/jetpack7/migloria/trans.html> (February 25, 2004).

3. "Crowds Grow in Miami," *ABC News.com*, April 13, 2000, <http://www.moreabcnews.go.com/section/us/DailyNews/elianscene000413.htm> (June 10, 2003).

4. "What They Said," *Miami Herald*, April 23, 2000, <http://www.miami.com/mld/miami/news/2046427.htm> (June 10, 2003).

5. Larry Flick, "Estefan Blends Caribbean Sounds on New Set," *Billboard*, May 2, 2000.

6. Jill Garneski Leon, "Gloria Estefan," *Celebrity Soup*, 2000, <http://www.celebritysoup.net/gloriaestory.htm> (February 25, 2004).

7. "The Unwrapping of Gloria Estefan," *Ocean Drive*, 2003, <http://www.beepworld.de/members27/gloria-latindiva-magazine/2003oceandrive.htm> (February 25, 2004).

8. Hans van Willigenburg, "Interview with Gloria Estefan," May 11, 2000, "Koffietijd" ("Coffee Break") on RTL4 (German television station), <http://www.geocities.com/sunsetstrip/stadium/8154/koffietijdtranscript.html> (June 21, 2003).

9. Entertainment Editors, "Gloria and Emilio Estefan to Receive Songwriters Hall of Fame Lifetime Achievement Award," *Business Wire*, June 12, 2001, <http://www.findarticles.com/cf_dls/m0EIN/2001_June_12/75471113/p1/article.jhtml> (February 26, 2004).

10. "Intimate Portrait: Gloria Estefan Gears Up for Next Year's Tour with a Stint at Caesar's Palace," *Review Journal*, 2003, <http://www.beepworld.de/members27/gloria-latindiva-magazine/2003reviewjour.htm> (February 25, 2004).

11. "The Unwrapping of Gloria Estefan," *Ocean Drive*, 2003, <http://www.beepworld.de/members27/gloria-latindiva-magazine/2003oceandrive.htm> (February 25, 2004).

12. Jerry Fink, "Estefan's 'Live & *Unwrapped*' Production Visits Caesars," *Las Vegas Sun*, October 09, 2003, <http://www.lasvegassun.com/sunbin/stories/archives/2003/oct/09/515719545.html?gloria+estefan> (February 25, 2004).

13. Doug Pullen, "Gloria Estefan Has a Lot of Creative Irons in the Entertainment Fire," *The Flint Journal*, August 29, 2004, <http://www.mlive.com/entertainment/fljournal/index.ssf?/base/features-1/1093791001 89550.xml> (February 25, 2004).

14. Ibid.

15. Michael Paoletta, "I've Learned to Live My Life in the Moment," *Billboard*, October 11, 2003, p. 22.

16. Karl Ross, "Anti-Foundation Spreads Gloria's Good Will," *Billboard*, October 11, 2003, p. 36.

17. "A Star in Every Sense of the Word," *Billboard*, October 11, 2003, p. 42.

Further Reading

BOOKS

Benson, Michael. *Gloria Estefan*. Minneapolis, Minn.: Lerner Publications Company, 2000.

Gonzales, Doreen. *Gloria Estefan, Singer and Entertainer*. Springfield, N.J.: Enslow Publishers, Inc., 1998.

Gourse, Leslie. *Gloria Estefan: Pop Sensation*. New York: Franklin Watts, 1999.

Marvis, Barbara J. *Famous People of Hispanic Heritage, Volume V*. Childs, Md.: Mitchell Lane Publishers, 1996.

Phillips, Jane. *Gloria Estefan. Women of Achievement Series*. Broomall, Pa.: Chelsea House Publishers, 2001.

INTERNET ADDRESSES

Gloria Estefan's official Web site, with news and music.
   <http://www.gloriaonline.com/>

Good source of articles, photos, lyrics, and links.
   <http://members.v3space.com/gloriaestefanlibrary/>

Good timeline of Estefan's professional life.
   <http://www.rockonthenet.com/artists-e/gloriaestefan_main.htm>

Index

Page numbers for photographs are in **boldface** type.

"1–2–3," 55

A

A Toda Máquina, 42
Abriendo Puertas, 83, 84, 99
Alma Caribena, 99, 100
"Along Came You," 90, 92
"Always Tomorrow," 76, 106
American Music Awards, 54, **60**, 61, 65, 70
"Anything for You," 55, 57, 78
Avila, Juan Marcos, 30

B

Bacardi International, 30, 42, 43
"Bad Boys," 50
Batista, Fulgencio, 13–14, 15
Bay of Pigs, **14**, 18, 21
Billboard music charts, 47, 48, 49, 63
Bongo's Cuban Café, 93
Bush, George H. W., 5, **6**, 65, 66, 77

C

Cardozo Hotel, 73
Caribbean Soul, **101**
Carpenter, Karen, 22, 50
Castro, Fidel, 15, **16**, 17, 18, 29, 82
CBS Records, 42, 45, 46, 47, 55
Clark, Maynard, 84–86, 87
"Coming Out of the Dark," 11, 69, 72, 78, 106
"Conga," 46–47, **48**, 50, 59, 83, 91–92

Crescent Moon Recording Studios, 73
crossover hit, 47–48
Cuba, 13–**14**, 15, 17–18, 28–29, 38–39, 41, 58, 77, 79, 82, 83, 94, 96–98, 100
Cuban Missile Crisis, 18, 19
Cuban refugees, 16–17, **40**, 83, 98
Cuts Both Ways, 6, 62, 63, 81

D

Dermer, Lawrence, 49
Destiny, 90, 92
Discos CBS International, 42, 45, 46
"Don't Wanna Lose You," 63
"Dr. Beat," 45–46

E

"El Ultimo Adios," 102
Epic Records, 46, 49, 55
Estefan, Emilio (husband), **6**, 28–30, **38**, 42, 43, **88**
  and Miami Latin Boys, 27–28, 30
  as band manager, 35, 43, 49, 51, 52, 57, 61, 62
  as producer, 43, 52, 57
  as songwriter, 43, 69, 102
  awards, 81, 102
Estefan, Emily Marie (daughter), 82, **88**, 89, 90, 92, 99
Estefan Enterprises, 72–73, 93

Estefan, Gloria, **6**, **38**, **88**
  and acting, 95
  and Cuban heritage, 38–39,
    58, 77, 79, 83, 97
  and Miami Sound Machine,
    30–31, **32**, 42–43, 46–**48**,
    51–52, **53**, 58–59
  anti-drug campaign, 6, 65,
    66–67, 68–69
  as mother, 40–41, 81–82, 89,
    92, 99, 100
  as role model, 52–53, 78
  as solo artist, 62–**63**, 64, 70,
    71, 72, 73, **80**, **91**–92, **94**,
    98–99, **101**, **104**
  as songwriter, 50, 54, 56–57,
    62, 69, 90, 93, 102–103
  as writer, 105
  awards and honors, 5–6, 52,
    53–54, **60**, 61, 64, 77, 78,
    79, 81, 82, 93, 99, 102, 107
  boat accident, 85–86
  bus accident, 8–11, **9**, 66
  business ventures, 73, 93
  childhood, 14, 17, 19–21, **20**,
    23
  courtship and marriage, 27,
    31–33, 36, 37–38
  early interest in music, 19,
    21, 22, **23**, 24, **25**, 26
  education, 26, 28, 37
  humanitarian efforts, 75–76,
    87, 89, 102, 106
  lawsuits, 64, 69
  operation and recovery, **12**,
    67–69, 70
  self-improvement, **34**, 35,
    56, **57**

  teen years, 24, **25**, 26
Estefan, José, 29, 38–40
Estefan, Nayib (son), 5, **6**, 7,
    8–10, 40, 58–59, 66, **67**, 69,
    82, **85**, **88**, 89–90, 92
"Everlasting Love," 81–82
Evolution Tour, 92, 103
Eyes of Innocence, 46

F
Fajardo, Gloria (mother), 14, 15,
    19, 21, 24–25, 26, 27, 28, 41
Fajardo, José Manuel (father),
    14, 15, 17–19, 21, 22, 24, 25,
    37–38, 40
Fajardo, Rebecca (sister), 21,
    26, 32
*For Love or Country: The Arturo
    Sandoval Story*, 100
Francis, Connie, 105

G
Galdo, Joseph, 49, 51, 61
Garcia, Enrique "Kiki," 30, 44,
    45, 46–47, 54, 61
"Get on Your Feet," 70
Gloria Estefan Foundation, 106
gloria!, 93
Gonzales, Elian, 96–98
Grammy Awards, 65, 81, 99, 107
Greatest Hits, 77

H
Havana, Cuba, **14**, 17, 79
Hold Me, Thrill Me, Kiss Me, 81
"Hot Summer Nights," 54
Hurricane Andrew, 73–75, **74**,
    76

I
"I Can't Stay Away from You," 55

Iglesias, Julio, 66
Into the Light, 70, **71**, 72, 92

J
Jerks, The, 49, 51, 61

K
Kennedy, John F., 18, 21
Klepper, Carmen, 68–69

L
Larios on the Beach, 73
Lebanon, 28, 40
Let It Loose, 55, 56, 58, 61
"Little Havana," 17, 59

M
Mi Tierra, 79, 81, 83, 99
Miami, Florida, **14**, 15, 16–17, 29, 53, 62, 66, 73, 75, 76, 96
Miami Latin Boys, 27, 28, 30
Miami Sound Machine, 42
Miami Sound Machine, 6, 30, 31, 33, 35, 62–63
    awards, 52, 54, 60, 61
    concerts and tours, **32**, 42–44, 46, 51–52, **53**, 58–59
    crossover success, 45–49
    hit records, 49–50, 55–56
Mottola, Tommy, 55–56
multiple sclerosis (MS), 24, 38, 40
Murciano, Mercedes (Merci), 28, 30, 44
Murciano, Raul, 30, 44
Music of the Heart, 95

N
Neuwirth, Michael, 11–12

O
Olympic Games, 90–**91**
Otra Vez, 42

"Oye Mi Canto," 64

P
Palmieri, Eddie, 64
Pan-American Games, 58
"Path of the Right Love," 106
Pope John Paul II, 82, 94
Powell, Colin, 75
Primitive Love, 49–50, 51, 55, 61

R
"Reach," 90–91,
Renacer (Live Again), 35
Reno, Janet, 97
"Rhythm Is Gonna Get You," 55
Rio, 42

S
Sony Music Entertainment, 64
Soviet Union, 17–18
Star Island, 62, 74
"Suave," 54

T
Tokyo Music Festival, 52

U
U.S. Customs Service, 21
United Nations, 77
United States Army, 21
University of Miami, 28, 37, 78
Unwrapped, 102–103, **104**

V
Vatican, 87
Vietnam War, 22, 24
Vigil, Rafael, 49

W
White House, 5–6
Who's Sorry Now?, 105
"Words Get in the Way," 50
World Trade Center, 102